FLORIDA

in

WORLD WAR I

FLORIDA

in

WORLD WAR I

JOE KNETSCH AND PAMELA GIBSON

THE
History
PRESS

Published by The History Press
Charleston, SC
www.historypress.com

First published 2021

ISBN 9781540246509

Library of Congress Control Number: 2020948630

Notice: The information in this book is true and complete to the best of our knowledge. It is offered without guarantee on the part of the authors or The History Press. The authors and The History Press disclaim all liability in connection with the use of this book.

CONTENTS

ACKNOWLEDGEMENTS

No one writes a nonfiction book alone. We were blessed with the assistance of a number of people who deserve recognition here. Our friend and mentor in publishing Dr. Nick Wynne has been a rock with advice and editing in this work. Our friends Cathy Slusser, whose fictional trilogy on the Atzeroth family, which covers much of the historical period of this book, is an inspiration, and Zack Waters, who loaned us his great-grandfather's portrait and gave us good advice on writing good history, and the Wednesday morning Koffee Klatch (Ron Block, John Depew, Martha Pytel, Jim Huffstodt, Tom Knowles, Burt Altman and Ed Stripling) put in their two cents (and more) on all of the chapters. Claude Kennison, whose collection and work for the state library is invaluable, has always been there when needed. The staff at the State Archives of Florida was—as always—very helpful in locating manuscripts, like the Bivens letters, that added the real human touch to this history. The staff at the Manatee County Public Library also lent their talents and time in assisting us retrieve information and preserve that county's rich history. Our good friend and longtime colleague Bill Howell was gracious enough to read every chapter and make very valuable suggestions. Our former colleagues and coworkers at the Department of Environmental Protection, Samantha Mercer, Jody Miller, Rod Maddox, Jorge Alonzo, Suzanne Lane, Linda Godfrey, Theresa Johnson, Callie DeHaven, Richard Malloy and many others have always encouraged us and bought our previous works. No historian would succeed in publishing if it were not for booksellers like our friends at My Favorite

Books and Midtown Reader (in Tallahassee) and the local Books-A-Million stores in our hometown. Our friends and colleagues in the Tallahassee and Manatee County Historical Societies have helped us in many ways, but most of all, they are friends, neighbors and inspirations. Although we cannot blame anyone but ourselves for the mistakes (if any), we do want to thank those noted and many more for their help, guidance and encouragement over the years.

Most importantly, for the production of this book and others, Joe would like to thank his wife, Linda Knetsch, for her help and technical expertise in getting this out on time. Without her, the book would still be in the talking stage. We especially want to thank her for her graciousness in catching influenza, which really inspired the final chapter, before the latest pandemic hit. She has put up with a lot, and we really do appreciate her efforts and love.

FLORIDA LOOKS AT THE WAR

1914–1917

I t has been assumed by many historians that Florida had little interest in the happenings of war-torn Europe at the beginning of the First World War. Some have even gone to the extent of stating that Florida's newspapers "largely ignored" the war in their daily coverage. Florida did have a rural population that may or may not have had a direct connection to the countries involved in the war, but that did not mean that they were ignorant to the events taking place in the Old World. The state had some very acute economic difficulties resulting from the war. Historian Wayne Flynt, in his excellent biography of U.S. senator Duncan Upshaw Fletcher, hit on this topic squarely, noting:

> *Fletcher's Florida constituents suffered heavily. Jacksonville's Schuler Cooperage Company, which exported wrapping paper to Europe, paid freight rates of twenty-three cents per hundred pounds in June 1914. Between August and late October, the company could not obtain shipping at any price....By December, the rate had climbed to forty-five cents or an increase of ninety-six percent. This rate drove the company completely out of the market.*

Flynt also noted that Pensacola's Chamber of Commerce had complained loudly that business at that port was languishing because it could not obtain shipping, "even at the piratical prices asked." Wherever exports were involved, including Florida citrus, the lack of shipping and the rising costs of shipping and insurance had a deep impact on the Florida economy. The impact of a short recession, which began around 1910 and lasted nearly two years, led to a sharp drop in tourism; Florida's tourism industry also felt the effects of World War I and did not recover until after 1918.

As one would expect, the lumber business fell off sharply, as historian Edward Keuchel clearly showed in his important article on the German American Lumber Company of Pensacola. To quote Keuchel's piece: "The outbreak of the war in the summer of 1914 virtually ended the Gulf Coast export business. Lumber at the docks was returned to the mills, and vessels ready to sail unloaded their cargoes. Prices on the export market dropped as much as twenty-five percent below the domestic prices as European demand decreased fifty-eight percent." The economic impact was immediate, sharp and totally unfavorable to Florida's industries. And all of this information was duly reported in the Florida press.

The amount of coverage that the newspapers of Florida gave to the Great War was quite large, and it was often very good. With the exception of the *Apalachicola Times* (a weekly publication), all of the newspapers in this chapter gave the war almost daily front-page coverage. The metropolitan newspapers, like the *Tampa Tribune,* the *St. Petersburg Daily Times* and the *Miami Herald,* frequently gave the war banner headlines. Pictures and maps on their front pages were also common methods for educating the Florida public. Throughout most of 1915, for example, the *Florida Times Union* (Jacksonville) averaged two and a half to three front-page columns of war news per day. The *Tampa Morning Tribune,* in March and April 1915, carried, on average, over three front-page articles per day. This average number of articles on the front page remained constant in May and June the following year. The St. Petersburg newspapers gave at least two columns of front-page coverage every working day. Much the same could be reported of the *Miami Herald* but slightly less for its rival, the *Miami Daily Metropolis.* The major metropolitan areas, therefore, were given good front-page exposure to the war news every day.

Smaller papers serving the more rural areas inland and on the coast also gave front-page coverage to the war. In 1915 and 1916, the *Daytona Morning Journal* consistently gave front-page space to the war. The *St. Augustine Evening Record,* sharing some of the same East Coast concerns as its colleague in Daytona, also gave front-page space to the war in Europe during these years. The tiny and financially strapped *Panama City Pilot* followed the pattern established by others by placing daily articles on its front page. Even during the hurricane of 1916, the war coverage remained on the front page. Along with the other newspapers of the day, the *Gainesville Sun* continually carried war news on its cover page. The weekly *Bradford Telegraph* also fell in line with its colleagues by running front-page items concerning the news from overseas. The state capital's newspaper, the *Tallahassee Daily Democrat*, also carried the war news on its front page, assuming the legislature was not in session. During the 1915 legislative session, it was difficult for the war to break onto the front page, but on occasion, it did appear. On both April 19 and April 20, 1915, however, one article did appear on the first page every day.

The front-page headlines and articles, however, do not come close to giving the entire picture of Florida's press coverage of the war. The interiors of every paper surveyed contained even more daily news, informative articles, pictures, maps, human interest stories, fiction and cartoons depicting the struggle going on in Europe and elsewhere. These papers brought to life the hardships and struggles of those caught in the maelstrom of war. Many papers featured some folksy observations like, "old man Neut Rality becomes more belligerent every day" or "the trouble with the average jingo is that he dispenses with the faculty of thinking." The sometimes fascinating "human interest" stories were often featured in the Sunday editions but, on occasion, crept into the daily coverage as well. The January 6, 1916 edition of the *St. Augustine Record* ran the story of "Why One German Fights No More: Killed French Soldier Who Had Wife's Picture in His Hand. Incident Wrecked Nerves." The *Miami Daily Metropolis* ran popular author Arthur G. Empey's thrilling article "How It Feels to Be Bayonetted" in its January 6, 1917 edition. However, most of the inside stories were often follow-ups to the front page or more direct battlefront news. Stories like "No Famine in Germany, But Food Saved," "William Thaw, American Aviator with French, Reported Killed" and "Czar Rewards Bravery of Women Who Enter the Army" represent the typical stories found inside the daily newspapers.

Cartoons figured into the mix also and made some of the more complex issues of the war easier for locals to understand—even if the view was a bit jaundiced. Both the *Miami Daily Metropolis* and the *Florida Times Union* ran the popular *Mutt and Jeff* series for most of 1915 and 1916. The duo of misfits were depicted in numerous situations while fighting on the front lines. One series cleverly explained the problems inherent in the unrestricted submarine warfare that had started in 1917. The "Scoop the Cub Reporter" series also carried numerous allusions to the war in its columns. Although they were intended to amuse, they also carried the messages of what the war was like overseas. Most telling, however, were the editorial cartoons, which were usually direct and pointed. Many of this genre would have made Thomas Nast proud.

The editorial opinions of the period were frequent and varied. In some cases, they reflected crosstown rivalries, especially in the Tampa Bay area and Miami. The *St. Petersburg Evening Independent* showed a marked pro-Entente stance throughout the period and often indicated its pro-preparedness feelings. The rival *St. Petersburg Daily Times* appeared much more skeptical of the news coming from Europe. Whether this was the result of knowing Great Britain had cut the Atlantic cables and was censoring the news reaching America is unknown, but it strongly backed President Woodrow Wilson's neutrality and heavily criticized Great Britain for its constant interference in American trade. In one of the more interesting photographs that was run in several papers, a "Russian spy" was allegedly taken into custody. The *St. Petersburg Daily Times* quickly pointed out the false nose and fake handcuffs used in the photograph and noted its propaganda interest. This newspaper also showed a photograph of Frenchman Jean Mario Caufolle (seen legless in the picture) and captioned the scene as "The Toll of the War." Unlike its crosstown rival, the *St. Petersburg Daily Times* also took an anti-preparedness slant in its editorials. In its May 5, 1915 editorial, the paper sallied forth against preparedness with the argument that it was too expensive and that "men in soft places in high rank" would increase the possibility of the United States entering the war. It clearly showed its colors when it noted in its May 29, 1915 editorial, "Great Britain cannot afford to lose the friendship of this country, especially at this time. In fact, no one of the belligerents can afford to lose it." To emphasize the variety of the region, the *Tampa Tribune* was openly critical of both Wilson and Secretary William Jennings Bryan but acknowledged that the United States may yet be forced to fight to defend its rights but that this would be a catastrophe if it did.

The rival Miami newspapers showed the potential bitterness stirred up by the preparedness campaign, which was headed by former president Theodore Roosevelt and General Leonard Wood. The *Miami Herald* illustrated a strong pro-preparedness argument. In its March 26, 1916 editorial, the paper noted its willingness to fight by telling its readers that it would back Woodrow Wilson if he wanted to fight over the sinking of the *Sussex* because the promises of the Central powers (Germany, Austria-Hungary and their allies) were "nothing more than scraps of paper." Americans should, in the opinion of the editors, have been willing to take up arms "to protect our rights." Throughout this period, the *Miami Herald* chided the Wilson administration as weak and indecisive.

"Only Free Peoples Can Hold Their Purpose and Their Honor Steady to a Common End and Prefer the Interests of Mankind to any Narrow Interests of their Own." (Woodrow Wilson)

Woodrow Wilson and flags. *Author's collection.*

The *Daily Metropolis* took the complete opposite point of view in its December 23, 1914 editorial, proclaiming, "America's neutrality is the greatest blessing the world could have just now, outside of peace among the warring nations....What is really needed is stricter enforcement of the neutrality laws, even to the detriment of our export trade." In its April 20, 1916 editorial, "Bunc in the Name of Patriotism," the paper criticized "business cheats" that hid behind the flag. A true feeling for the deepness of the *Daily Metropolis*'s stance on neutrality can be seen in its January 3, 1917 editorial, "The Nation Should Be Trained for Peace." Here, the editors wrote, "[Americans should] train the youth of America to understand the true causes of the war in Europe—show them that the war in Europe is a hideous example of what the worship of commercialism can produce. Train them in this truth that war is murder and that the United States is big enough to refuse to be terrified by any trumped up 'war scare.'" The *Daily Metropolis*, in this case, was not intimidated by the rival *Miami Herald* or its northern rival, the *Fort Lauderdale Sentinel*, which was also a supporter of preparedness.

Other editorial comments throughout the state showed a similar division of opinion. The *Daytona Morning Journal* from March 2, 1915, said in its editorial, "The Call of Blood," "The hour is at hand for all peoples in the

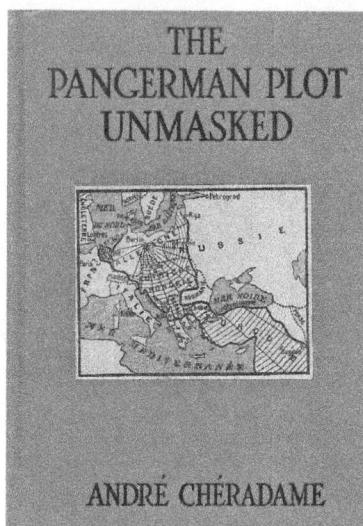

THE
PANGERMAN PLOT
UNMASKED

ANDRÉ CHÉRADAME

The Pangerman plot unmasked.
Author's collection.

United States to use extreme caution and great forbearance in discussing the conflict in Europe, lest a spark ignite the powder which is to blow our neutrality to the four winds." The *Gainesville Sun*, early in the United States' pre-entrance years, put the question that was on the minds of many into the open: "With nearly all Europe engaged in the greatest war of the ages, what becomes of the old argument that to be prepared is the best guarantee of peace?" North of Gainesville, through Waldo and into Starke, the *Bradford Telegraph* continued the call for preparedness throughout 1915 and 1916. Meanwhile, though mildly pro-Entente, the *Tallahassee Daily Democrat* announced its true feelings through its headline on October 12, 1916: "Asking Billions for the Slaughter of Humanity."

There is little consistency in the editorial opinions that were found in the newspapers of the state except that almost all were united in the desire to keep America out of the war and support the neutrality of the Wilson administration, weak as it may have been. It was the method of maintaining the neutrality—not the final goal—that divided the editors of the Florida press. As Christopher O. Coddrington, the president of the Florida Press Association, noted in his open letter to President Wilson, "The world is war mad. If it can be honorable to do so, the United States should stay out of the maelstrom. The press of Florida as a unit will uphold you in your trying position." (This important letter appeared in the March 13, 1915 edition of the *St. Petersburg Times.*)

Editorials in the newspapers were not the only venue for putting opinions in front of the Florida (and American) public. Of all the means to get the message across to the average Floridian, the motion picture may have been one of the most important. It was relatively new at this stage and a true fascination for those in towns lucky enough to have a local movie theater. As noted by British scholar M.L. Sanders, "The cinema had the greatest impact of all pictorial propaganda, possibly through its novelty." Early in the war in Europe, Wellington House (the headquarters of much of British propaganda) recognized the cinema as the "Bible of the working classes," the groups who were probably least affected by novels, books and pamphlets. Many of the films sent to the United States depicted wartime conditions in Europe, and some concentrated on front-line action. Jacksonville was treated to footage of German and Austrians fighting on the eastern front (against Russia) on September 9 and September 10, 1915. *At the Front with the Allies* made its Florida debut in Miami at the Paramount Theatre in January 1917. St. Petersburg viewers were thrilled by the exploits of J.A. Marion as he told the story of his Canadian light infantry battalion losing 975 men of its 1,100 who began the assault, and this included some pictures of the grisly scenes. Daytona was also visited by the thriller *Our Enemy Spy*, a truly "great war feature in three parts," according to its advertisement. Probably the most widely viewed movie was the *Battle Cry for Peace*, which was based on Hudson Maxim's Defenseless America series. This motion picture visualized an unprepared America being invaded by an outside force closely resembling Germany's soldiers in uniform. This feature was viewed in Tallahassee in October 1915 and in Tampa at the Strand Theatre on July 3 and July 4, 1916.

The Defenseless America series closely followed the popular series by novelist Irving Hancock. Hancock produced a series of similar books, including *At the Defense of Pittsburgh: The Struggle to Save America's Fighting Steel Supply*, which depicted very German-like soldiers marching into Pittsburgh in its illustrations. Fiction writers, most well known in America, were recruited by Wellington House to write stories and books from the British point of view. Sir Gilbert Parker headed this effort and used a unique method of distributing the products of his colleagues. He personally wrote to his American acquaintances and friends, sending them copies of the books, pamphlets and other publications produced by his colleagues, including Sir Arthur Conan Doyle and Rudyard Kipling. Nonfiction books almost flooded American bookstores and libraries. They included such writings as the popular Guy Empey's *Over the Top* and *First Call*, Ian Hay's *The First Hundred Thousand*, Colonel James Fiske's *In Russian Trenches* and more academic tomes,

In the defense of Pittsburgh.
Author's collection.

The Author just before Leaving for Home.

"Over the Top." *Author's collection.*

such as Henri Hauser's *Germany's Commercial Grip on the World* (which featured German investments in Latin America and made the claim that Guatemala was little more than a German colony without a flag). Price Collier produced another of these volumes early in the war titled *Germany and the Germans from an American Point of View*, which also implied the rivalry for trade and German expansionist desires. More blatant was André Chéradame's *The PanGerman Plot Unmasked*. The title of this propaganda work gives its content away up front. Many of these efforts were backed by Wellington House but not all. Books and pamphlets were important to the British and German propaganda efforts, but without a large, urban population, the impact may not have been what Parker and others wanted in Florida.

In this era, the pulpit played a vital role in informing the public of national and international events. Dr. H. Rains, for example, preached his "peace sermon" at the Christian Church on March 29, 1915, which received a favorable review by the *Miami Herald*'s church reporter. A favorite Miami visitor—and later resident—was former secretary of state William Jennings Bryan. The "Great Commoner" gave a speech on

January 14, 1916, at the Men's Club of the Presbyterian Church titled "Christianity at Fault if It Cannot Secure a Substitute for War." Many ministers of the Florida Sunday School Association urged their young flocks to support the association's part in raising one million nickels to aid those injured by the war, including soldiers on both sides. Not as charitable was the Reverend B.E. Tallent's sermon in Gainesville, which asked the question, "Is Emperor Wilhelm II the Beast of Revelations?" Like most public institutions, the churches kept the war in front of their flocks and generously gave their own points of view.

Many groups in Florida also played active roles in letting their peers know about the war. Particularly active was the Florida Federation of Women's Clubs. The club's first vice president, Dr. Mary B. Jewett of Jacksonville, led the statewide campaign to protest the sale of munitions to the belligerent nations as a hopeful means of ending the war. The local St. Petersburg club, known as the Women's Town Improvement Association, which was led by Mrs. Herman Merrell, spoke on behalf of the drive and noted that two million American women would be heard on this issue. In the Redlands, south of Miami, Mrs. William Krome led the Women's Club's drive to sell prized grapefruit in New York to raise money "for the benefit of the European war sufferers." In this drive, the club successfully raised $1,525 for the cause. The crowning achievement for the federation's peace drive came when Governor Park Trammell declared Tuesday, March 18, 1915, as "Peace Day" on behalf of and at the bequest of the Florida Federation of Women's Clubs. In addition to the statewide campaigns, the federation chapters held classes, discussion groups and other social and educational meetings throughout the state.

Kaiser Wilhelm II as king of Prussia. *Author's collection.*

There were also clubs that appealed to the more partisan interests of Floridians. German American clubs could be found in St. Petersburg, Tampa, Jacksonville, Daytona and Miami. The Jacksonville club was emboldened enough to call itself the "Kaiser Club" and even held a "stew" in celebration of von Hindenburg's successful drive into Russia following the Battle of Tannenburg. When Herman Ridder, the editor of the *New York Staats Zeitung*, died in early November 1915, the Daytona German

American Society held a special meeting to honor his memory, and the *Daytona Morning Journal* ran a eulogistic editorial. The *Miami Herald* informed its readers of the formation of a Miami German club, which held that "its object [was] the promotion of sociability among its members and the dissemination of information concerning the German people and culture." On March 27, 1915, the same paper ran an advertisement announcing a free lecture on the "History of the European War" by Dr. Anton Meyer-Gerhard of the Imperial Colonial Ministry of Berlin. Meyer-Gerhard was a special envoy for the German ambassador to the United States, Count Johann von Bernstorff, who also headed the German espionage and sabotage efforts in America. The speech given by Meyer-Gerhard was attended by over six hundred people according the *Herald*'s account the following day. In the spirit of cooperation, the Tampa German Club gave time and a meeting space to the United Jewish Women's Relief Society, which offered aid to Jewish victims of the war and, to some extent, money to aid in their resettlement in Jerusalem. War relief was also the aim of the Daughters of the Empire, who held their annual Christmas sale to raise money for the relief effort.

Military preparedness did not leave the headlines; it remained an active topic and led to the formation of a number of new organizations. On March 1, 1915, the *Tampa Morning Tribune* announced the formation of the American Legion "to protect the country." This group was founded to promote military preparedness and national defense. Jacksonville stalwarts clamored for the chance to get involved with the naval militia, which soon boasted that many ex-Annapolis graduates had joined. Upriver, in Palatka, the "Gem City," not to be outdone by its downstream rival, a company of men was soon organized to join the state militia. The national guard units from Florida engaged in extensive recruitment during this period, primarily to get their units up to the size permitted by legislation. Also, under the capable leadership of then-captain Albert Blanding, the national guard organized itself for its tour of duty along the Mexican border to chastise Pancho Villa in 1916. The National Defense Act of 1916 made the national guard the "first line reserve" for the regular army; this added to the prestige of the unit and drew in many young recruits who were anxious for service. The national and state drive for preparedness actually aided in the improvement and expansion of the Florida National Guard. The Second Florida Regiment, which had gone to the Mexican border, returned in the spring of 1917, just in time, as historian Robert Hawk noted, to find themselves mobilized for overseas duty. The Mexican adventure served them well as training for what lay ahead.

On the other side of the preparedness controversy, Florida held its widely publicized "Peace Convention" in Orlando during the first week of May 1915. At this convention, Dr. J.J. Hall spoke on the "Uselessness of War." Militarism received rough handling from speaker Arthur D. Call. A Miss Deadrick (no first name given) of Rollins College spoke of women and their roles in the crusade for peace. The Peace Convention received little publicity outside of the articles in the Jacksonville-based *Florida Times Union.*

Throughout the period under consideration, the war was the major topic for discussion. The *Apalachicola Times* reported on April 10, 1915, "It has been a matter of comment in this county why warships failed to sail up the Dardenelles, capture Constantinople and make the Turks behave themselves." Mrs. Guy A. Pride led the South Jacksonville Book Club in a discussion of "America's Interests Abroad." The Miami Current Events Club, which met monthly, discussed preparedness and women's roles in it. On January 14, 1916, the Belgian Relief Committee of Miami held a card party, which had forty tables and netted sixty dollars for the effort. No imagination is needed

A recruiting poster for the navy, labor and army. *Author's collection.*

to surmise what the main topic for discussion was there. Nor would it have been much exercised at the April 7, 1916 meeting of the Daughters of the American Revolution (DAR), Everglades chapter. The next day, the DAR sold Belgian flags on behalf of the relief efforts—April 8 being King Albert's birthday. On and on read the reports in the society pages for the entire era. Society was interested, the "man on the street" was interested, and to have avoided discussions and writings about the war would have required an intentional effort.

Florida was very well informed about the events going on in Europe during the first three years of the Great War (1914–1917). As noted earlier, the daily reporting was substantial and contained many details of the fighting, the relief efforts, accounts of life under the bombs, et cetera. Florida's news media covered the events of world importance with verve and intelligence. It offered differing opinions to its readers and gave breadth to the coverage. No one can assume that Florida—rural as it was in 1917—was not well informed. Overall, the people of Florida were well served by the press of the day and were offered a variety of views and news stories. It should also be noted that when the men were called to war, Florida was ready. The men and women who volunteered their services could count on the folks back home being aware of what they were about to face. It was a proud moment in Florida's newspaper history.

FLORIDA'S LIBRARIES' GROWTH AND WORK IN WAR AND PANDEMIC

1914–1919

As social agencies, libraries have historically reflected contemporary values, and World War I was no exception.
—Arthur P. Young, "World War I, ALA and Censorship," Newsletter of Intellectual Freedom, July 1977, 95.

Never underestimate the power of women who read. By 1914, nearly forty years since Melvil Dewey began his system of organizing library collections, public libraries were just beginning to enjoy the stability of municipal support and funding. Professional librarians selected and organized collections, and the new American Library Association (ALA) supplied library guides for book selection. There were never enough trained librarians to fill positions, especially after Andrew Carnegie's public library buildings appeared, but most municipal libraries grew out of ladies' groups that supported elite and popular reading. In libraries throughout the South, most librarians were local women of good character who knew books. Libraries and collections reflected the majority population: white, middle class and Protestant. Small branch libraries were evolving in larger cities to serve an inquisitive public.

Most librarians who held top positions in state and national library organizations were men, and women dominated the local scenes in library and civic clubs. After April 1917, libraries lost many of their male staff members to conscription and enlistments, which left more women at the helm of local and state libraries.

Florida was still in the process of transitioning from local ladies' library associations to larger municipal libraries as money from city governments and the Andrew Carnegie Foundation became available for building programs. These building programs continued throughout the war, although an increased demand for funding for war relief agencies, food conservation programs, Liberty Bond drives and Red Cross activities made raising local funding for a Carnegie Library increasingly difficult.

Florida's first nonprivate libraries were created in 1845, following the granting of statehood, and they were considered parts of government branches or departments. The Florida Supreme Court Library and Florida Department of State, which later included the state's Division of Libraries, were the first. Amid the Third Seminole War, in 1856, the Florida Historical Society was founded, and it began collecting items relating to the state's archaeological Spanish, French, British and Seminole history. A fire later seriously damaged that collection, and parts of it were trashed when Union forces occupied St. Augustine during the Civil War. Not until 1903 did the Florida Historical Society begin to gather new collections for a library of Florida history.

Post-Reconstruction libraries were usually founded by women's clubs and village improvement associations. Jacksonville was the major port and railroad center in a state that was largely destroyed by the Civil War. Jacksonville's library service began with May Moore and Florence Murphy and their small library and literary association in 1878. Members created a free public reading room in the winter of 1878–79 for Florida's winter tourist season. The first librarian was James Douglas.

In 1883, the association reorganized under a new name, the Jacksonville Library Association, and built a "neat one-story frame building" with a steep roof along Adams Street. This building was replaced in 1894 by a building that the library shared with the Board of Trade and the Elks Club—probably for reasons of space and cost following the Panic of 1893. Libraries soon realized that sharing space allowed more people to become acquainted with libraries, which would build a base of support for public library service. This second building was destroyed in the May 3, 1901 great Jacksonville fire, which destroyed most of the city. Other small-town and village libraries were created prior to 1900 and became the founding libraries for the later countywide systems. Leesburg got its library in 1883, Winter Park in 1885 and the Walton County Public Library System began in 1886. Monroe County's library at Key West began in 1892, and West Palm Beach's library opened in 1894. Cocoa, Dunedin and Palatka's libraries all began in 1895, and Bartow's library opened in 1897.

The first library in Brevard County was a one-room building rented for five dollars a month in Cocoa Village in 1895. Local dues were one dollar, and citizens donated books and furniture. By 1900, there were four small libraries across the county in Cocoa Beach, Eau Gallie, Melbourne and Titusville. Ladies took turns as volunteer librarians.

Library service on the south bank of the Manatee River began in Bradenton in 1898. The *Manatee River Journal* reported on December 15, 1898, that a six-hundred-volume circulating library was located in Mr. W.C. Lightfoot's Fruit and Vegetable Store. The offer of the day was "buy one book for 50-cents or 75-cents and for 10-cents or 5-cents, you can read all the other books in the set."

Around the same time, Julia Fuller set up a small circulating library with a shelf of books in the millinery department of Mrs. Bass's Dry Goods Store, operated by George Wallace. In this rental library, books were loaned for five cents a week. With the funds, Fuller purchased more books for this collection. This library was very popular, and the collection grew rapidly. Soon, the collection moved to the store of Miss America Sudbury. By 1904, the collection had grown to the point where a separate building was needed to house it.

The Bradenton's Ladies Village Improvement Association formed around 1900 and established a library committee. When pharmacist Dr. John C. Pelot donated to the library, the library committee incorporated as the Bradentown Library Association to give it the legal status it needed to give the community a proper library. Unsuccessful at gaining funds from Carnegie's library program, in 1907, Mrs. T.J. Bachman loaned the ladies $500, interest free, for the construction of a one-room concrete building with a porch across the front. The Village Improvement Association Library opened in December 1907. Mr. Lucien Stone served as a librarian without pay and was assisted by other volunteers.

Palmetto, on the north bank of the Manatee River, was a winter vegetable and citrus shipping point in the 1890s. A Village Improvement Association (VIA) was organized by the ladies on March 30, 1900. Mrs. J.A. Lamb, a member of the town's founding family, was the president. They held ice cream socials, bazaars and excursion boat trips to Tampa to raise funds for various projects. One of their chief interests was the library, which was then located above S.B. Black's Grocery Store on Palmetto's Main Street. This collection was transferred to rooms above the Harrison-Dickie Drugstore, and ladies served as volunteers in the library, which was open two days a week.

Top: Ladies Village Improvement Association Library, circa 1900–1910. *Courtesy of the Manatee County Public Library.*

Bottom: Interior of the 1914 Palmetto Carnegie Library. *Courtesy of the Manatee County Public Library.*

In 1912, the Palmetto Library Association was formed, and control of the VIA Library was vested in a board of directors, with Belle Fuchs as librarian. The library remained above the drugstore until the City of Palmetto assumed control in 1913. The collection continued to grow and was moved into Palmetto's City Hall, making the need for more space obvious to city councilmen. The collection was moved to the new Carnegie library when it was completed in 1914.

As Europe went to war and the United States declared neutrality, the small town of Palmetto, its library still in the city hall, arranged for Mayor B. Whitehead to write to the Carnegie Foundation in New York about obtaining a construction grant. On January 14, 1914, after months of correspondence between Mayor Whitehead and Andrew Carnegie's personal secretary James Bertram, a $10,000 grant was approved. Palmetto agreed to provide $1,000 per year from taxes and provided a fifty-foot-by-one-hundred-foot lot on Main Street. The new building was opened to the citizens of Palmetto on December 29, 1914.

Orlando's first library was a circulating library provided by the Sorosis Club for its members in the old armory building but later moved to the

Knox building on the corner of Pine and Court Streets. In May 1920, N.P. Yowell of the library committee got the city council to put a proposition for a public library before the city's voters. The citizens voted 414 to 22 that they were willing to tax themselves $1,000, or 10 percent of the library's cost, to pay for a proper library building. A retired police inspector from New York, Captain Charles L. Albertson, offered the city his collection of books in November 1921 on the condition that it furnish a suitable library building, name the facility for him and make him a lifetime library superintendent. Like Carnegie's libraries, the city would have to suitably maintain the library. Albertson's offer gave Orlando the push that it needed. Other pre–World War I Florida libraries included the 1902 Eustice facility, the rebuilt Jacksonville Public Library in 1903, Hudson's library in 1904 and Titusville's library, which opened in 1906. St. Petersburg's library opened in 1910, and Lake Worth and Zephyrhills's libraries opened in 1912.

J.P. Morgan bought out Carnegie in 1901, and with John D. Rockefeller and one hundred other firms, he founded U.S. Steel. The sale created the world's first billion-dollar holding company. Carnegie's share of the sale came to $255 million. Carnegie used his wealth to build public libraries across the United Kingdom and America. By the time of his death in 1919, Carnegie had funded 2,811 free public libraries. He felt he had gained knowledge from libraries that helped him become a captain of industry, and he offered the world a way to acquire this knowledge. In Florida, Carnegie gave $208,000 to build 10 public libraries and 4 academic libraries. The Carnegie Corporation, which was in charge of Carnegie's philanthropic activities, introduced standard application forms, criteria for judging applications and businesslike processes for approved funding.

Carnegie also stepped forward after the 1901 Jacksonville fire to replace the destroyed 1894 Jacksonville Public Library with $50,000 toward construction. As with all Carnegie projects, there were strings attached. He did not construct buildings that would deteriorate due to lack of care or become abandoned due to lack of funding. Cities receiving Carnegie libraries had to provide proper building sites and budget 10 percent of Carnegie's donation per year as library support for staffing, supplies, books and periodicals. Only responsible communities could receive a grant.

Jacksonville accepted the challenge and put the matter to a vote. The result was 640 to 627 to accept Carnegie's grant. Jacksonville's 1903 City Ordinance established a free public library and a library board led by Duncan Upshaw Fletcher, a two-term mayor of Jacksonville and, from 1909 to 1936, the longest-serving United States senator in Florida's history.

Jacksonville's two-story-tall Carnegie library built from limestone and copper was designed by Prairie School architect Henry John Klutho, who was responsible for rebuilding much of the burned city. The new library opened on June 1, 1905, with George Burwell Utley as its librarian and with 8,685 books. This was the first tax-supported library in Florida.

Bartow began its quest for a library in March 1897, when the town formed its library association, headed by Dr. G.H. Perrine and Mrs. E.W. Codington. Entertainment events were held to raise the funds for the books, shelving and other necessary materials. Florida's cattle baron Ziba King allowed the newly established library to operate out of a building he owned rent free until a permanent place could be found. With the community strongly supporting the idea of a Carnegie library grant, a grant was successfully applied for, and the new library opened in 1911.

By 1914, Bradenton's little VIA building had become overcrowded. The ladies of the Bradenton Women's Club again approached the Carnegie Foundation to get a grant. In order to qualify for Carnegie funding, no other library could exist in the municipality, so the ladies closed the VIA Library and sold the lot and building. Because the Carnegie Foundation only dealt with government bodies that had taxing power, successive Bradenton mayors, E.B. Rood and C.A. Birney, supported the application. It was not until Mrs. Bachman took over the effort, however, that the effort produced positive results. The new building opened on October 12, 1918, just a month before the armistice.

St. Petersburg boasted a large community of outstanding women, including some who were physicians and businesswomen and others who had artistic and literary talent, including Jerome Cable, the pen name of St. Petersburg author Katherine Bell Tippetts. Through their efforts, the city received a Carnegie grant of $17,500 to create the Mirror Lake Library

Bradenton's 1918 Carnegie Library as seen in 1928 and 1929. *Courtesy of the Manatee County Public Library.*

in December 1915. Bellona Brown Havens, an accomplished poet and magazine writer, became the "redoubtable mistress of the St. Petersburg Reading Room and Library" and its 2,600 volumes.

The efforts to get a Carnegie Library in West Tampa were greatly aided by the friendship that Hugh C. Macfarland, the former city attorney, had with the steel magnate. In 1907, Macfarland resigned his legal post to become the head of the city's public works. When the citizens of West Tampa "heartily endorsed" the library in a referendum in 1913, Macfarland made the required application, used his personal relationship with Carnegie to add weight to the request and saw it approved. The West Tampa Library opened on North Howard Avenue at a cost of $17,500.

A Tampa referendum was passed to accept Carnegie funds to build a library on October 29, 1912. This was Tampa's second referendum since 1902. After years of wrangling and dispute, the second vote to accept the Carnegie offer was passed. Carnegie's gift of $50,000 funded the construction of a library, and on June 30, 1915, the city accepted the new building on East Seventh Avenue. The Tampa Public Library began service in 1917 with a donated collection of 3,800 books.

Smaller Carnegie libraries, which were funded with $10,000 grants, were founded in Gainesville and Clearwater. Both were functional and needed in these small but growing communities.

Among the 108 college libraries constructed nationwide through Carnegie gifts, the first three of Carnegie's Florida academic libraries were built in 1905 with a wide range of construction costs. In Martin County, Fessenden Academy's library was built in March 1905 at a cost of $6,500. Little is known about this library except that it was built almost entirely by Black laborers.

The Carnegie Hall Library at Rollins College was the second college library completed in Florida. Its construction cost was $20,000, and the building had over eight thousand square feet of space. The school, which served both "the grandchildren of abolitionists and confederate soldiers in about equal numbers," fit Carnegie's profile of equality of library service. The required $20,000 for the building was granted after W.W. Cummer, a school trustee from the board of the Jacksonville Carnegie Library, and other trustees wrote on the school's behalf. It took two years, but the necessary matching funds were finally raised. The building was completed and dedicated on February 18, 1909, and it served the school until 1951. Securing matching funds for the Carnegie grant and guaranteeing operating funds took a tremendous effort from backers of the Rollins library. The college's president William

Fremont Blackman noted their struggle when he wrote, "Our college is in the poorest of states, remote from all centers of wealth and population, and our friends have strained themselves to the uttermost in the effort to raise the $230,000 in two years." Of this sum, $200,000 was used for an endowment, and the additional $30,000 was used to erase debt.

The third college library completed in Florida was the Library of the State Normal and Industrial School for Colored Students at Tallahassee. In 1905, a fire destroyed Duval Hall, the school's main building and library. Aware of the Carnegie grants, the alumni association applied for funds. After receiving a $10,000 grant, the library opened in 1908. The City of Tallahassee refused to accept funds for a library because Carnegie required that all the libraries he funded serve all patrons, without regard to color, race, religion or immigrant status. That proved too much for the leaders in the state's capital city.

A fourth Carnegie library was built at John B. Stetson University in DeLand. Stetson was famous for the hats that still bear his name and made him a fortune. He founded the college that bears his name in the early 1890s, maintaining a close watch over his school until his passing in 1905, the same year the grant for the library was approved. This library was opened one year later, in March 1906, at a construction cost of $40,000.

Andrew was not the only Carnegie to assist in advancing library services. Mrs. Carnegie visited popular author Kirk Munroe near Miami in the late 1890s. During a meeting of their Pine Needle Club, she met the author's wife and asked what the club needed most. Learning of their great need for books, Mrs. Carnegie soon donated enough books to the club that a small building had to be constructed for them. The land for the building was donated by Ralph Munroe. The Coconut Grove Library Association was incorporated in October 1900, and the new building was ready in March 1901.

The assassination of Archduke Ferdinand and his wife in Sarajevo in 1914 sent shockwaves around the world, and rival nations went to war as the situation quickly escalated out of control. Words became bullets as alliances were invoked and armies took to the field. American newspapers were quick to send reporters to the front lines, and the public experienced the drama and suffering in the trenches.

Floridians, too, closely followed these events, and some even took action to alleviate some of the pain and suffering. By early 1915, over three hundred thousand school children had signed a "peace petition" that was to be sent to the ambassadors of the warring nations by Dr. B.T. Trueblood of the

American Peace Society. This petition appeared on the front page of the *Daytona Morning Journal.* The *Miami Herald* prominently noted the peace sermon given by Dr. Rains at the Christian Church in downtown Miami. The Daytona paper ran an editorial praising the Sunday School Association for trying to raise a million nickels for the aid of soldiers in Europe. The same paper, on February 17, 1916, noted the savage attacks on libraries in the greater Chicago area, including the Newberry, with the headline "War Fanatics Cut and Mutilate in Libraries." Exactly why these attacks took place remains unclear.

Sympathy for Germany did appear in some cities and segments of the population. In Florida, Daytona, Tampa and Miami, there were active German clubs, and they tried to get their homeland's side of the story out to the public. The *Miami Herald* noted in its March 27, 1915 edition "Prominent Germans Form a German Club," with the object of promoting friendship among its members and "the dissemination of information concerning the German people and culture."

American libraries were instructed by the American Library Association (ALA) to be unbiased in their thoughts and sentiments. Librarian Corinne Bacon called for librarians to "avoid all bias, religious, political or economic," and to "have books on both sides of a question." Few libraries were able to accomplish this goal. As soon as the war was declared, the ALA put out a list of books that should be avoided. Effective British propaganda and control of the transatlantic cables made neutrality impossible. By the end of the war, the ratio of pro-Allied to pro-German books in American libraries was around fifty to one. With growing suppression of anything pro-German and harassment of anyone suspected of being anti-American, most librarians had little chance of enforcing the ideals put forth by the ALA.

Library construction in Florida boomed between 1914 and 1918. Pensacola Naval Air Station saw the opening of a new library in 1914, and the Florida Department of Agriculture's library at Gainesville, Tampa's Carlton Fields Law Library and libraries at Clearwater, Tampa and Vero Beach all opened new facilities in 1915. Libraries were opened at Largo, Tarpon Springs and Umatilla in 1917. Even as Americans fought the influenza in 1919, New Port Richey and Lake Wales enjoyed the openings of new libraries.

Early libraries unquestionably practiced censorship. It was felt that libraries should uphold the contemporary moral standards of their communities. There was a belief that trashy books—religious or political polemic volumes, dime novels or comic books, obscene works or those with a prurient interest—would inflict long-term damage on young minds, so separate children's rooms were preferred. The goal of libraries was to facilitate community cultural uplift. Libraries—it was felt—owed a duty to their taxpayers.

The Gilded Age, between 1876 and 1900, saw a massive growth in the printed materials that were available to the public. Carnegie's library building program came at a time of mass urbanization, expanding industrialization and rising literacy rates. With a few exceptions, such as Jacksonville and Tampa, Florida either missed or was spared many of these powerful trends. Early Florida libraries supplied moralistic children's books that were common to the Victorian era, along with romantic stories for the ladies that were set in medieval England, Scotland or Victorian London and sometimes contemporary New York. Some classical authors and revered authors, such as Charles Dickens and Mark Twain, also appear in early Florida library accession records.

By the beginning of the Progressive Era in 1900, city libraries offered more varied fare to their readers. Books were more liberal in their tones and advocated for cultural tolerance and understanding. As motion pictures created other outlets for leisure time, opinions were shifting away from the rigid moral judgements of Victorian Era Florida. Censorship policies changed with time. More nonfiction on scientific topics joined religious and agricultural offerings on library shelves. Tampa, which was home to Cuban, Spanish and Italian tobacco workers, had lectors who read a wide variety of literature, from romance novels to the latest political and revolutionary works, for often illiterate cigar workers during the workday.

As libraries became staffed with professional librarians, most had collections that were usually neutral on most subjects that were not deemed "inappropriate" for young or uneducated minds. Obtaining materials on both sides of an issue was necessary for an informed citizenry in a democracy. The mere existence of a community book collection was powerful enough to change and inform people's ideas, attitudes and tastes. During the years of American neutrality in World War I (1914–1916), information on all sides of the war was gathered. In Europe, the *Library Journal* noted funds for libraries were diverted to pay for the war. American libraries got involved in and allowed fund drive meetings that were held to aid Belgian refugees, Belgian libraries and wounded or disabled soldiers.

Florida's public libraries collected books to inform local readers and to meet patrons' demands during the war years. A survey of American libraries showed that much more information on England and France in books and

Left: A Boy Scout liberty bond drive near the Manatee County Courthouse. *Courtesy of the Manatee County Public Library.*

Right: Anton Kleinoscheg Whitaker of Sarasota's pioneer family in 1918. *Courtesy of the Manatee County Public Library.*

periodicals reached the public, while very little information on Germany, Austria-Hungary, Serbia or Russia was collected. English-language newspapers were almost entirely pro-Allied. Other than Tampa's *La Gazeta*, which was printed in Spanish and Italian, there were few foreign-language newspapers in Florida library holdings.

German American families in Manatee County were viewed as pioneers and were respected members of the local society. They were considered southern rather than foreign. The Atzeroth family, originally from Bavaria, had settled on the north bank of the Manatee River and on Terra Ceia Island during the Second Seminole War. "Madam Joe," the matron of the family, grew the first coffee in the continental United States and received a ten-dollar gold coin from the president for her work. The Kleinoscheg family of Graz, Austria, came to the United States in the mid-1800s and began farming near Sarasota. They intermarried with the Sarasota postmaster Abbey's family and the Whitaker family, the founding family of the area. One descendant of the family, Anton Kleinoscheg "A.K." Whitaker, served in the U.S. Navy during World War I. Because the Kleinoschegs had been integrated into local society, they were not considered foreign; they were considered part of the upper class and cultured.

Many books and pamphlets on the European war were donated to U.S. and Florida libraries, thus sparing small libraries' budget expenditures on acquisitions. The most prolific publisher was Wellington House; it

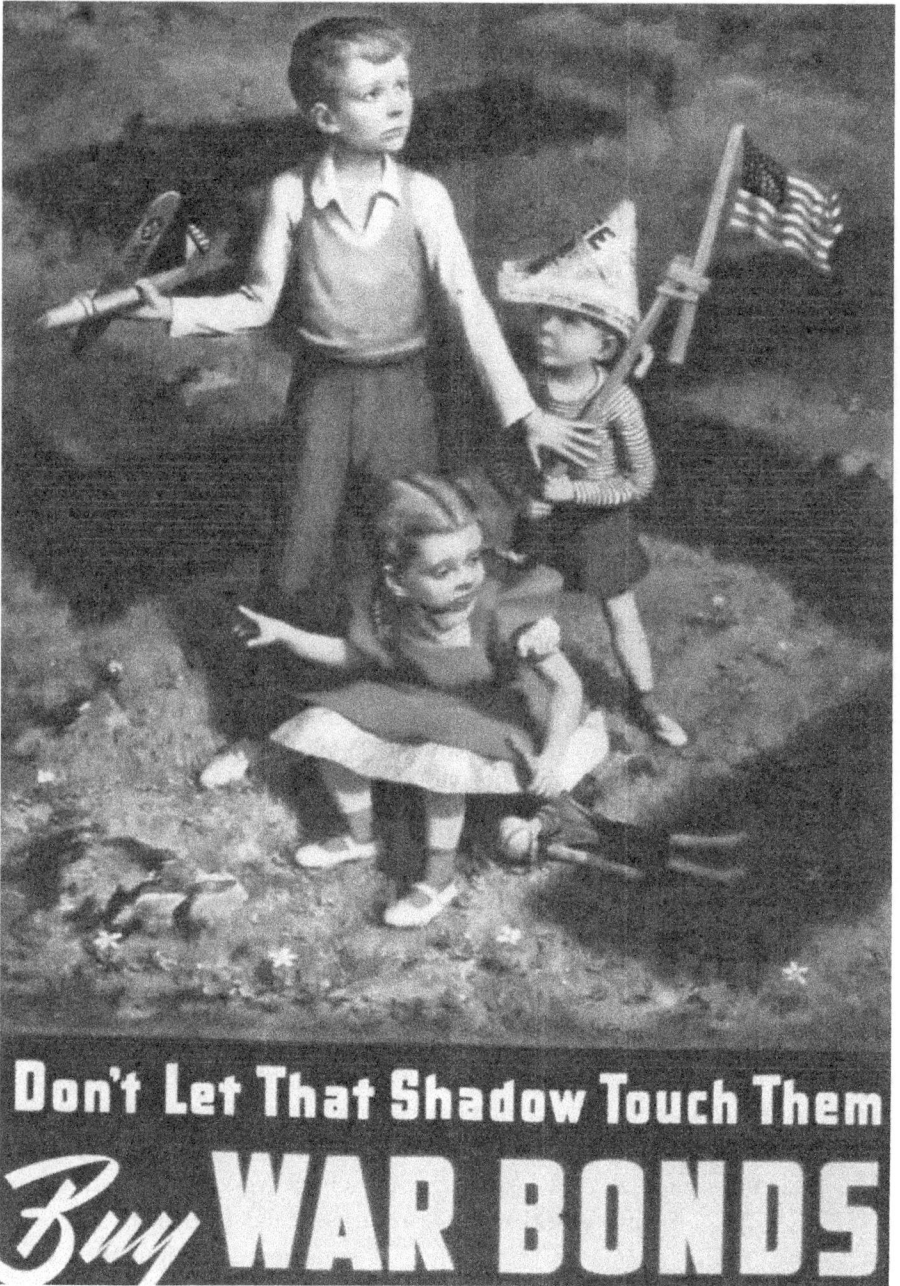

Fear of the German enemy was the precursor to later War Bond drives. "Buy War Bonds."
Author's collection.

posed as a regular publisher but was actually the propaganda arm of the British government, and it supplied much of the free materials. There was a strong and growing interest in books on European history and politics, while the appetites of Florida's lady readers for medieval, Tudor- and Regency-era romantic novels continued. Librarians who were trying for a balanced and neutral approach to the war found it "well-nigh impossible" to do so.

At least forty U.S. organizations published and circulated anti-German literature during the period of American neutrality, and their efforts continued with even greater fervor after the United States declared war. The federal government formed a "committee on public information" to present the official American view of the war, and it urged libraries to supply these materials in order "to make the war a personal challenge" to the general public. News sheets and pamphlets were distributed to ten thousand libraries. After these materials were donated, most of the books, magazines and newspapers in Florida libraries were anti-German.

The position of the American Library Association on intellectual freedom underwent a reversal with the entry of the United States into the war, and it asserted that libraries could not guarantee intellectual freedom in the same sense as the First Amendment because they had budget constraints, politically appointed management and real people as staff members and patrons. It was necessary, therefore, to "exercise some screening capacity over the wealth and quality of available material." In effect, efforts at neutrality in libraries ceased with the declaration of war. Local tax-based funding tied local libraries quite closely to the needs and opinions of their local communities.

This war was portrayed to the public as a crusade for democracy. Although those in library professions continued to discuss balance, the consensus was, "Now we are at war, we are not neutral. We go with the will of the people. But we still have a duty to collect this literature for historical reasons." Formed in 1917 with Herbert Putnam of the Library of Congress at its head, the ALA's War Service Committee decreed that "ordinary functions must yield to extraordinary demands of the times." Putnam declared that it was the library's "primary duty to act as an agency of patriotic publicity."

While librarians were adamant about the idea of "spreading the gospel of the library's value to society," they were also caught up in the excitement about the war and the idea of national sacrifice. Florida readers, library patrons and library staff members, like most Americans, simply went "war mad" under the deluge of patriotic calls to duty.

The ALA quickly promoted the military and food conservation programs of the U.S. government and worked to incorporate libraries onto ships and into army training camps. Over five thousand libraries accepted these wartime book donations, and over 1,200 library workers served in libraries on military bases in the United States, on ships and overseas in camps. This work transformed the ALA from a "sedate, professional association" to a public service organization. Of the 411,505 books purchased by the ALA—mainly on technical subjects from carpentry to firearms—385,310 were shipped overseas. There were 2,100,000 total books sent from Florida bases like Key West, Jacksonville and Pensacola to the battlefields and hospitals of France.

As local newspapers sought out slackers, hoarders, pacifists and various subversives, libraries checked the list of banned books from the newspapers and removed the listed books from their shelves. None of the banned titles listed were found in the 1918 accession book of the Bradentown Carnegie Library. Book distribution remained the main function of librarians during the war.

A poster designed by Charles Buckles Falls from World War I in which a marine in a uniform and a tin hat with a USMC canteen on his hip and rifle over his shoulder holds a tall stack of books in his arms became popular with Americans. The wording of the "Books for Sammies" campaign read, "Books wanted for our men in camp and 'over there.'" Florida libraries took part in the national book drives, which were held in September 1917, March 1918 and January 1919. Many of the donated books were old, damaged and had suffered from the pre-air-conditioned Florida climate. The ALA requested contributions from the public to buy multiple copies of new books directly from the publishers. By October 4, the Library War Council had reported to Secretary of War Newton D. Baker that it had placed $800,000 of the money in the hands of the treasurer for that purpose.

On October 2, 1918, the *Florida Times Union* used a large portion of its editorial space to urge its readers to "Give books to the soldiers." The public was reminded, "Three million men would like to have the privilege of reading them, as they are not situated where they can buy them, and many cannot afford to do so if they were given the opportunity." Liberty loan drives, food conservation posters and literature from various patriotic organizations and government agencies were displayed and distributed through local libraries. The *Florida Times Union* from September 2, 1918, gave the Fourth Liberty Loan attention on its editorial page. It said, "We must stint and economize

Camp Johnston Library, circa 1918. *Author's collection.*

and save—and it is our patriotic duty to loan these savings to the government and buy War Savings Stamps or Liberty Bonds—or both."

With large government expenditures at Jacksonville's Camp Joseph E. Johnston for training men and the city's shipyards, local newspaper editors felt that a bond quota of $6 million from Jacksonville's residents was not unreasonable. Large advertisements, such as one that appeared on September 29 from the Liberty Loan Executive Committee, helped send the people into the banks and post offices, where bonds and war savings stamps were sold. All Florida newspapers carried such advertisements on a regular basis, and Florida libraries made the newspapers available for their patrons.

Suggestions for war work by library staffers included creating exhibits, displaying posters and books, presenting lectures and distributing government publications, such as those published by George Creel's Committee for Public Information (CPI). Libraries with meeting rooms or extra space also hosted Red Cross meetings and registrations. The Red Cross was the most favored group mentioned in Florida newspapers and was well known for its drives for medical funding, nurses and aid for war refugees and civilian hospitals near war zones during the years of American neutrality. When the United States entered the war, the Red Cross went into the battlefields, offering assistance in military hospitals, counseling and assistance to wounded soldiers and other services.

Growing and preserving food, wheatless and meatless meals and other conservation measures were promoted by the information available at libraries or in the extension classes held there. Such activities helped increase the production of critical supplies for American troops, Allied nations and refugees. The U.S. Food Administration was formed under Herbert Hoover immediately after the declaration of war. By May 19, 1917, Hoover had an extensive program in place. Involving agencies and institutions already in place and using newspapers for advertising, local libraries for distributing information, free recipes for alternative food sources and people who came together for voluntary conservation, the Hoover plan reached all Americans. If a person picked up a pamphlet in a library or read about food conservation in a newspaper or magazine at a library, they were participating directly in the war effort.

The Hoover program seemed to galvanize mothers, cooks and gardeners and spur them to greater efforts. Book displays on cooking, preserving and gardening, in addition to pamphlet distribution and newspapers with the latest reports and lectures for local ladies' canning clubs, were ways the libraries aided the war effort. Rural Florida offered many agricultural and gardening possibilities, and canning clubs held meetings. Libraries provided books, magazines, pamphlets and recipes that featured the state's produce while advocating the "Food Gospel of Conservation."

The *New York Times* announced in a page-one story that control of food by the government was to begin on November 1, 1917, in an effort to eliminate unreasonable profits by growers and grocers, speculation by investors and depletion of food sources by hoarders. An appeal in June 1917 asked American housewives and women to sign pledge cards to try to use one pound less of bread per week; it persuaded two million women to pledge within the first month.

The food conservation program was an unparalleled success. A January 1919 summary of the work of the Library Section of the Food Administration recorded 127 "library letters" sent, 1.5 million pamphlets and leaflets distributed and 600,000 posters posted in prominent places. It also featured hundreds of photographs of library food exhibits and a variety of maps showing critical food situations. These powerful messages critical to the nation's military success were effectively delivered by America's libraries.

With the arrival of the Spanish flu, few cities were quick enough to take precautions to prevent its spread. There was a war, and citizens felt that the economy and war efforts had to carry on despite the ravages of some unknown disease. Military camps did not close, although many collapsed under the ferocious onslaught of influenza. Those urban areas that acted quickly had far lower infection and death rates than cities that were slower. For many cities in which schools closed, libraries were still open, and children were brought to the libraries and often left there to read or amuse themselves while their mothers went to do Red Cross or war work. Florida's newspapers carried news of closing orders for various cities, including court and government closings, but libraries were never mentioned in the lists. While the continued operation of America's libraries could be viewed as a tribute to the value of libraries and reading, the failure to appreciate that "there is a time for everything," including closing libraries, raised the infection rate during the war.

During World War I, American libraries underwent a growth in community action, passing from small ladies' clubs to organizations that could fulfill a role in national service. It was an exhilarating time, when public libraries found their niche as a new municipal function from which local citizens came to expect certain services. Librarians were considered skilled professional gatherers and distributors of war news and information—better than any other municipal source. Library rooms served as meeting places for clubs and war service groups that provided practical instruction in a variety of fields and information on politics. With many men away from home in service, libraries led the campaigns for food production and conservation; thus, they acquired community standing and quasi-governmental authority. Ladies who had watched the quiet little club libraries become large municipal libraries became willing volunteers, assisting the professionally trained librarians who were practicing skills in selecting, acquiring, cataloging and organizing their collections.

Florida saw a steady increase in the number of local and special libraries. Displays, children's programs and available meeting rooms brought people into these libraries. Once there, they found news about the war and local news in a variety of newspapers, wartime pamphlets and handouts, as well as books that they could check out and read. Book donations continued throughout the war and into the postwar years. The libraries of Florida represented a part of the state's contributions to the war effort, to the unity of the nation and to the elevation of the patriotic spirit of the country.

3

GERMAN ESPIONAGE IN THE UNITED STATES: WHAT HAPPENED IN FLORIDA?

The German American Lumber Company had a mill in Florida's Panhandle near St. Andrews, and that could only mean one thing: the Germans were planning a submarine base in the Sunshine State. On April 15, 1917, the *St. Andrew Bay News* reported, "And we have German spies among us....Not many months since a German was in our bay in a small craft, ostensibly on a sketching tour. His sketches are undoubtedly now in the possession of the German raiders." Although it took nearly a year, the German American Lumber Company was seized by the United States government and later sold to a group of American investors. St. Andrews Bay was not the only location in Florida to house German espionage activity, and many Floridians feared submarine attacks along the state's coasts before too long. As for the St. Andrews Bay lumber company, its president, "Prince" Hoffkamer (H.G. Kulenkampff), who was from somewhere near Bremen, Germany, was actually there as a result of directions from the German Foreign Office, which allegedly supplied the funds for the enterprise. Arrested and taken to Fort Oglethorpe, Georgia, where he was interred for the rest of the war, the "Prince" was subjected to intense questioning about his relationship with the foreign office. Although he did not confess to any direct connection, a Tallahassee newspaper reported that he was undoubtedly associated in some way with this branch of the German government.

Even supposedly innocent fishermen, like Harry Michalson, an alleged "alien enemy" who was caught fishing within a zone near Mayport from which aliens were barred from entering, were suspected of espionage activities. Taken into custody and questioned by authorities, he stated that he was trying to make a living as a fisherman and had no evil intent. Michalson's story was not believed, and he was arrested and imprisoned on federal charges, not just a local charge of trespassing. The local newspaper reported, "In the same connection, it is stated that there are a number of such men working as fishermen all around the coasts of the United States. Important facts have already been gathered along this line it is stated." The paper's declaration was a tacit warning that residents should be wary of all fishermen who were of alien status and might be reporting strategically important information to the enemy.

The First World War was the first "total war" to be fought by Americans, and they made every effort to prevent defeat. The enemy, at any time, could try to bring about dissension and revolution, and strikes by sympathetic—usually anti-British—labor unions reduced arms production through sabotage and the spread of defeatist propaganda. General John J. Pershing, who was commanding American forces in Europe, was very aware of such threats at home and viewed the Italian loss at Caporetto as a result of socialist defeatist propaganda, which sapped the fighting spirit of Italian soldiers. The morale of individuals on the home front clearly mattered a great deal. The Military Intelligence Division (MID) of the U.S. Army made it clear in its pamphlet *Propaganda in Its Military and Legal Aspect* that the grand strategy followed by the enemy was to cut the army off from its base by stopping the flow of munitions and guns, food supplies, reinforcements and comforts from home. Anything that weakened moral support for the American cause was to be fostered among the disaffected. Everything possible to safeguard America's military preparations and to discourage enemy agents from attempting to damage the country's morale and industries or debauching the soldiers was to be done. All-out wars called for all-out campaigns to stop the enemy at home and abroad. One of the biggest problems for the United States was the small amount of infrastructure that existed to support antiterrorism efforts or to carry out counterintelligence or counterespionage operations. The end of the Spanish-American War saw the curtailment of the Office of Naval Intelligence and what became the army's Military Intelligence Division. This forced the military to start almost from scratch, and they had to do it quickly.

Are hysterical headlines and sensational reporting worthy of serious consideration as historical evidence? When put into the context of German sabotage and espionage of the day, they are. In two recent volumes, *The*

Fourth Horseman: One Man's Mission to Wage the Great War in America and Howard Blum's notable *Dark Invasion: 1915: Germany's Secret War and the Hunt for the First Terrorist Cell in America*, the true nature of the perceived threats by contemporaries seems very real indeed. In Robert Koenig's *The Fourth Horseman*, the author documents the terrible tale of Dr. Anton Dilger's attempt to cut off the supply of American horses and mules to the armies of the Allies by introducing anthrax and glanders germs into livestock scheduled for shipment overseas. These deadly germs decimated thousands of horses and mules, which crippled the war effort.

Dr. Dilger was born near Front Royal, Virginia, in 1884 and was sent to Germany for his early education. He attended the University of Heidelberg, graduated in 1909 and received his doctorate in 1912. One of Dilger's fields of study was microbiology and germ culture, which came in handy when he returned to the United States in 1915 as an agent in America working for the Prussian War Ministry. From the basement of his Chevy Chase, Maryland home, Dilger involved his brother (willingly) and sister (unwittingly) in the plot. Access to the holding areas for the livestock of the remount service of the United States Army was nearby in Virginia, a short drive away and easily attained. Dilger's efforts soon paid off, and the remount service faced an outbreak of disease among its herds of animals destined for Europe.

From Virginia, Dilger made his way to Kentucky, and when an outbreak occurred in Kentucky herds in the summer of 1917, authorities automatically assumed it was the work of German agents. Individuals with German backgrounds, like Dilger, were watched closely. He soon left Kentucky and, on orders, headed to Mexico to try to instigate a possible invasion of the United States from that country. It was a mission destined to fail from the beginning, and Dilger soon fled to Spain, where he died under mysterious conditions. It is suspected that the Germans killed their own agent because he knew too much about the biological warfare he attempted, the German machinations in Mexico and certain espionage assignments in South America. Some of his activities were known and reported, but most remained secret; however, Dilger's diabolical plot to spread disease among the remount service's horses and mules was discovered and made newspaper headlines. News of his subversive activities added to the hysteria spreading across the country in 1917 and 1918.

Blum's recent work details the activities of a ring of saboteurs that operated out of New York and were followed and hunted by Captain Tom Tunney and the NYPD bomb squad. Tunney and his team were America's first line of defense at the country's busiest harbor. Local efforts, like those of Tunney and his men, were essential because the United States had no national intelligence system in place, with the exception of a few naval and military attachés who were attached to diplomatic missions overseas. The United States was totally unprepared to take any action against saboteurs or anyone else bent on damaging U.S. trade with the Allies; thus, the largest port city had to provide the immediate protection of American shipping and storage lest the enemy destroy the immense profits that were then being made by American industry and—later—farmers trading with the Allies, England, France, Belgium, Russia and Italy. Tunney's team was the front line of America's defense.

The United States had only a rudimentary concept of communications security and no cryptology agency to break enemy diplomatic and military codes. "Still more remarkable," Michael Warner observed, "no federal statute forbade peacetime espionage and sabotage." Congress had, as usual, failed to provide adequate funding for the rapid expansion of ONI or MID. Indeed, Tunney's closest ally in the fight against German sabotage was the British naval attaché in Washington, Captain Guy Gaunt, the head of Section V who was working through Franklin Polk, his liaison with the Wilson administration.

When the war broke out in Europe, nearly one-third of the United States' population was foreign-born or had parents who were born overseas. This was the group—especially the German- and Austrian-born portions—that was targeted by propaganda from all sides. Although the target groups were large, most were loyal to their new home and had left Europe because of its lack of land and opportunity. The German propaganda was very heavy-handed and academic, which made it ineffective. Most could not be counted on to assist the Central powers in covert operations against the United States. British propaganda efforts fared better because as soon as the war was declared, the Atlantic cables connecting Germany and the United States were cut, thus ensuring the dominance of the British viewpoint in most newspapers, which relied on the cable for coverage of foreign events. British censors further bolstered the Allied propaganda efforts by eliminating about three-quarters of the dispatches from American correspondents stationed in Germany and the Austro-Hungarian Empire.

In addition to the German-speaking immigrants, authorities in the United States were concerned about the Irish, Indian (British Empire) and African American groups within the population who were also targeted by German propaganda and intelligence. Radical groups like the Industrial Workers of the World (IWW or Wobblies) only added to the mixture of those who were potentially against the war, pro-German or simply anti-English. Complicating matters even further, many German-owned ships and their crews headed to the nearest neutral ports, especially those that were in the United States when war broke out. Many that were never returned to German service were incorporated into the U.S. Merchant Marine under new identities. Identifying the potential saboteurs among the crews of these ships proved to be a very difficult task, especially on the docks of New York.

The fact that there were many German organizations in the United States before the war was well known, and as early as August 1914, Dr. Charles J. Hexamer, the president of the National German-American Alliance, was writing and complaining to President Woodrow Wilson that the Colt Armory Company was violating the president's neutrality declaration by making machine guns for the Canadian government and demanding an investigation. The secretaries of the Erie and Detroit branches of the same organization also wrote complaining about the shipments of coal into Canada to fuel British battleships, which was another violation of neutrality in their view. When news was released in late November 1914 that Charles M. Schwab had negotiated a $50 million arms contract in Europe, the National German-American Alliance was livid and demanded something be done to halt this "illegal" traffic. Assistant Secretary of State John E. Osborne told Hexamer and the other complainers that large numbers of Americans believed that any restrictions on the trade, barring new legislation, was not warranted by international law and custom. The official position became, "If the articles were contraband, the enemy of the purchasing government had the right to intercept them, but, failing that, the United States was under no obligation to prevent the sale." Neither the president, Congress nor any department had specific authority to halt such traffic. It was a very open-ended policy that required no enforcement by the United States. But the fact remained that Great Britain controlled the seas and continued to blockade the ports open to the Central powers, so American neutrality worked to the exclusive advantage of Germany's enemies. Appealing to Washington to do anything to halt this lucrative traffic was an exercise in futility.

The result of this policy was to make the United States a de facto supplier of all things to the Allies and to make America a creditor nation in the process. Prior to the war, the United States had been a debtor nation, always with an unfavorable balance of trade. With the outbreak of war in Europe, the United States became the largest creditor nation in the world. Its army was miniscule compared to those fighting on the front in France, Belgium and Russia; its navy was growing but was not in the same class as Great Britain or

Germany. But without the burden of a large and all-consuming defense budget, the United States became the "richest" country in the world. With Germany on the sidelines in Latin America and other underdeveloped areas, Americans were free to exploit their rival's absence, and they quickly took advantage of the situation. As a result, the United States' policy of neutrality was that it was not neutral toward Germany and the Austro-Hungarian Empire. What would be the response of those countries be?

One of the most obvious responses by the Central powers was to sabotage and prevent the passage of war materials to the Allied countries. The burden

Naval attaché Captain Karl Boy-Ed. *Author's collection.*

of supervising German sabotage activities fell first on Count Johann von Bernstorff, the German ambassador to the United States. He was summoned home in early 1915, and instead of being shuttled to the Foreign Office, he was deposited at the doorstep of Section 3B, the military intelligence bureau for the general staff. He was curtly informed that he was then to be the chief of espionage and sabotage efforts in the United States. The count had no experience in any of these kinds of operations, but Section 3B supplied experienced assistants to help him.

They assigned Captain Franz von Papen, who was later the head of the German postwar government but who was then serving as a military attaché to Mexico, to head the sabotage efforts. He had the assistance of Captain Karl Boy-Ed, the naval attaché to the United States. The finances for the covert activities were funneled through Dr. Heinrich Albert, the commercial attaché to the United States. This small, elite group of men directed the most dangerous threat to the United States ever—or it would have been had it succeeded. The conspirators set up offices on Broadway and in the Wall Street area of New York City and began recruiting volunteers and other enlistees to carry out some of their plans.

The small group hatched numerous plots to sabotage ships, critical infrastructure and munitions plants in 1915 and 1916. One of the first plots was an attempt to blow up the Welland Canal, which allows ships to bypass Niagara Falls, to shut off trade with the interior of New York and

Canada. The man who was chosen to lead the attack on this key waterway was Horst von der Goltz, who had been trained in the German espionage school by Walter Nicolai, the chief of the German intelligence bureau, Abteilung III b, who assured von Papen that he could do the job. His primary difficulty was in recruiting trustworthy men who were willing and able to assist him in the enterprise. He first tried recruiting three German sailors who had been sequestered in the port of New York as neutrals and looked promising, but none of them had the right attitude or aptitude that was needed to successfully carry out the mission. To replace them, von Papen supplied him with three more unemployed German sailors as recruits. After going over the plans and securing the necessary explosives, the men took the train to Buffalo. As they surveyed the canal, von der Goltz's crew grew impatient and doubtful about their mission. The canal appeared to be guarded by troops along its entire route. The crew deemed it nearly impossible and returned to their hotel in Buffalo. Seeking to find a vulnerable opening for the attack, von der Goltz took to the air to scout out the canal's defenses. When he got back to the hotel room, he found his crew had abandoned him. He returned to New York City to report his failure to von Papen, who grew angrier and angrier with every word von der Goltz spoke. He finally lost his temper completely and stormed out of the room. He later demanded the recall of von der Goltz. It was a harbinger of things to come.

Captain Franz von Papen, an ex-German military attaché. *Image from* History's Greatest War: A Pictorial Narrative, *1919.*

Perhaps the most insidious plotter was a former Harvard professor who was on the lam after murdering his wife. Erich Muenter was a creative and deceptive individual who had fled south to Texas and began his life all over again. He eventually wound up teaching in Texas and appeared to all to be an educated, articulate man with a new young wife from the region. Muenter, under his new name of Holt, decided he could assist the German cause by assassinating financier J.P. Morgan Jr., who was heavily involved in financing the British war effort through loans and letters of credit.

On July 2, 1915, Holt (Muenter) left a bomb in the U.S. Capitol that did some major damage to the interior. He fled from this caper and made his way, by train, to New York. There, he took the local Oyster Bay Line out Matinecock Point and caught a cab driven by Arthur Ford. Holt told Ford to drive to the Morgan estate, where he left the cab and walked boldly to the front door of the Morgan mansion. He introduced himself as Thomas Lester of the Society Summer Directory. He then insisted on seeing his "old friend" Morgan. The butler, a man named Physick, was taken aback by this brash stranger, and when Holt insisted on seeing his "old friend" Morgan, he directed him to the library. After failing to find Morgan in the library, Holt proceeded to the breakfast room, where the financier was eating with his wife. As Holt entered the room, he leveled two revolvers at Mrs. Morgan. Morgan reacted instantly and threw himself at Holt. Weighing some 220 pounds, Morgan was able to pin the much smaller would-be assassin to the floor. During the scuffle, Holt managed to get two shots off, hitting Morgan in the abdomen and left thigh. Undeterred by his wounds, Morgan held Holt while his gardener and butler pounded him into unconsciousness. The local police arrested Holt and then conducted a search of his hotel room, where they found dynamite and another revolver. He admitted to planting the bomb in the Senate building, and he also admitted to placing another device on an undisclosed ship. One day later, a cargo ship burst into flames after a device similar to the one that was used in the Capitol exploded. While in custody, Holt disclosed the location of a trunk filled with unexploded bombs and bomb-making materials.

In New York, Tom Tunney and his team went to work to uncover, once and for all, the network of German spies and saboteurs who were being funded and promoted by the German embassy. Holt was questioned about the network and promised to reveal everything he knew on July 7, which was only a few days away. On July 6, however, Holt unsuccessfully tried to kill himself by slashing his wrist. Frustrated by his failure, Holt was later successful when he leapt to his death as his cell door was opened. Although Tunney got only limited information from Holt, the event focused the nation's attention on Germany's continued efforts to disrupt American commerce and politics.

The major break in the case for Tunney and his men came with the fortuitous forgetfulness of a commercial German attaché who momentarily left his briefcase on a bus. The briefcase was retrieved by Frank Burke, one of Tunney's most trusted agents, who had been tailing the attaché for hours. The briefcase contained information on most of the financial dealings of the German network, including the details of payouts to agents, financing for various pro-German newspapers and the purchase of questionable office supplies. The ledger also contained the names of members of the

German network, including the leader of their dock operations. In addition, information on the placement of "cigar" bombs that were designed to hamper British and American shipping was discovered. Reacting quickly, Tunney ordered his men to round up the individuals who were named in the ledger and other documents for questioning. Under pressure from Tunney's agents, most of the spies broke very quickly. Although many of the rank-and-file members of the network were arrested and imprisoned, the leaders of the network, including von Papen, Dr. Heinrich Albert and Karl Boy-Ed, had diplomatic immunity and were ordered to leave the country. Tunney and his team had broken the German spy ring and nearly ended the sabotage in the Northeast. The chase had been long and hard with many frustrating incidents, like the explosion at the Black Tom and the sinking and damaging of several vessels that were leaving New York for Europe.

The Black Tom explosion and the massive destruction it caused in the New York Harbor area made headlines everywhere. The original plan to destroy the Black Tom facility, the nation's largest docking area for war goods, was drawn up by Franz von Rintelen before he left on recall to Berlin. The execution was left to Paul Hilken, one of the German agents who was working under von Papen with Dilger. An unlikely spy, Hilken was described as a nervous type who always seemed to be on the edge of a breakdown. He never did break down, however, and he never lost his love for espionage. Working with Frederick Hinsh, Hilken finalized the plan and passed it on to Kurt Jahnke and his associates, Lothar Witzke and Michael Kristoff, who put it into play.

On the night of July 29, 1916, small fires were seen coming from the docks at Black Tom near the location of *Johnson Barge No. 17*, which was loaded with one hundred thousand pounds of TNT. The barge was not supposed to be there, but the owner wanted to avoid dockage fees at other docks. Jahnke and his team set up the incendiary devices at different points along the dock. Security guards who worked for the dock's owners tried to put out the fires, but they were too extensive. The men fled and called the Jersey Fire Department. Around 2:00 a.m., the fires set off a major explosion; it was so powerful that it created a shock wave equal to an earthquake with a magnitude of 5.0 or 5.5 on the Richter scale. Windows shattered as far as twenty-five miles away, and in Times Square, glass flew out of the skyscrapers; shock waves were felt as far as ninety miles away, and people were rocked out of their beds by the huge blast. Hundreds of people were hurt, mostly by flying glass, and seven people were recorded as dying as a result of the explosion. Some of the shrapnel from this blast was even lodged in the skirt of Lady Liberty. To this day, access to the torch is forbidden due to the damage done by this blast.

The Black Tom explosion was the last major successful sabotage attempt by the German network. Most of those who directed the affairs of the network were soon ordered out of the country or were arrested and imprisoned for the remainder of the war. On February 1, 1917, the German government announced the resumption of unrestricted submarine warfare, a move that helped push Woodrow Wilson into declaring war with the Central powers.

The coast of Florida offered numerous opportunities for spies to enter the country without notice. Suspicious schooners, trawlers and other watercraft were constantly sighted in the Gulf Stream and other coastal waterways. Even Assistant Secretary of the Navy Franklin D. Roosevelt sent a warning to the Office of Naval Intelligence, stating:

> *I have been told by a man just back from Florida, who knows parts of the Florida coast pretty well, that one Gus Muller has been taken into the Naval Coast Defense Reserve as a lieutenant and that while there is nothing definite against him, he will bear watching. He was either born in Germany or here of German parents; also, that a boat named Joyeuse, last reported at Fernandina, will bear watching.*

Did any of this espionage ever reach Florida, and what was the reaction of the state's population? The *Miami Metropolis* was very active in reporting the numerous arrests of spies in the New York area. One alleged spy, Walter Ortolph, was arrested in Tallahassee after it was reported that he was looking over maps in a remote field and "using some kind of wireless instrument." By September 3, the charges had been dropped due to insufficient evidence. The same newspaper ran a number of stories on the alleged bomb plot in New York was headed by Dr. Herbert Kienzle and one Robert Fay. The two were charged with conspiracy to blow up a munitions ship, and their pictures appeared in the November 12 edition of the paper. After receiving a tip from British authorities, the German-owned Hamburg-American Line came under scrutiny by the federal government, and three members of the line's main office were charged and tried in New York with illegally shipping war materials on the company's passenger liners. They were also charged with chartering coaling and supply vessels, loading them with supplies and then transferring the contraband to waiting German ships, a violation of the neutrality of the United States. It is not known if this was part of the *Etappendienst*, the German Secret Naval Supply System, or a rogue operation. By the time the United States entered the war, such stories were daily fodder for Florida readers.

Editorials trumpeted the need to destroy the spy rings that appeared to be springing up around the state. The *Milton Gazette* bitterly asked how Walter Sporrman, an officer in the German army and alleged spy, could easily find employment that allowed him to attempt to blow up the Hamilton Naval Base. "What," the Panhandle newspaper asked, "is the matter with our people that they are so criminally careless in taking on men they do not know and concerning whose antecedents they make no inquiry?" In the *Tallahassee Weekly Democrat*, the headline for January 25, 1918, read "Impurities Found in Candy Sent to Our Soldiers: Powdered Glass Found in Candy Sent to American Boys on Naval Ships." The same paper reported that a suspected spy had been killed in Miami when he was being questioned by two aviation inspectors. The spy, Robert W. Clapp, was being followed for some days prior to his death under the suspicion that he was a spy. The *Cocoa Tribune* published in its July 20, 1918 edition the story of a local man, Ralph Rubin, who was credited with discovering a German spy while on his leave from his base in South Carolina. On the train he was taking home, Rubin was approached by an inquisitive stranger who aroused his suspicions. He told the conductor, who arranged for the train to be met by several men, including a uniformed policeman. The suspected spy attempted to flee, and after following him through several cars, he was apprehended as he exited the train. The man admitted that he was a German spy and that he was trying to get information about military training camps. So excitable were Floridians by this time that when one northern German American tourist, who was caught without proper clothing for a cold snap, blurted out, "Damn such a country as this," he was immediately arrested under the Espionage Act. In Pensacola, a German American was severely flogged by a citizens' group; he was then ordered to shout out "To Hell with the kaiser" before being politely ordered to leave the state.

Labor troubles were also attributed to the influence of German agents and caused the *St. Petersburg Times* to wonder why the death penalty was not instituted to halt the strike of lumbermen in the spruce forests of the West. The spruce was intended to launch America's large force of newly designed airplanes. Of course, the reporting of a German plan to attack the United States via Mexico roused the Florida population to a fever pitch. This was a result of the publication of the infamous Zimmermann Telegram in early 1917. Luckily, not all the news was bad and foreboding. Key West reported that there were no Germans landing in the island city in April 1917; after all, the city had organized one thousand men to defend the city from a German invasion. There had been earlier reports of some sort of attack from a German submarine on the city, which later proved to be false. Such were the reports from the fair state throughout the United States' action in the First World War.

Cade Cover's thesis, "German Covert Operations and Abandoning Wilsonian Neutrality" (Wright State University, 2018), is worth a look when researching how Woodrow Wilson's public and private conversations and speeches added to the nation's atmosphere of fear and dread. By examining the president's speeches, private correspondence and recorded conversations with associates, it is clear that Wilson added to the general hysteria of the day. By frequently labeling the nation's German American population as enemy aliens—with the caveat of noting that the enemy was the German government—Wilson created the impression that any German American should be suspect. The passage of the Espionage Act and other legislation added to the overall suspicions held by the majority of America's citizens. Wilson's approval of the creation of the American Protective League did not lessen his tacit approval of the suppression of the German American minority. Wilson's public and private exhortations are worth examining in light of some of the tragic consequences of that time.

4

THE FORESTERS AND THE CONSTRUCTION OF THE FRONT LINES IN FRANCE

I t's not often that a movie inspires a history to be written; however, after viewing the film *1917*, it was clear that the design of the setting and the recreation of the battle scenes were excellent. The front line was one of trenches that stretched from the Swiss border to Belgium. Each trench was constructed using wood from the forests of France, England and Scotland. (Very little came from the United States because of the country's late entry into the war and the lack of transport vessels to bring the wood to Europe.) The trenches, with their bombproofing, scaling ladders, duckboards, trench mats and reinforcements (revetting), were made entirely of wood. The consumption of the forests of England, Scotland and France was enormous. By 1917, an additional problem arose on the front lines: there was a severe shortage of men to harvest the wood needed for the trench works and hundreds of other applications. Although the movie does not depict the role played by the foresters, the amount of wood displayed in the war scenes gives viewers a relatively accurate picture of the prominent role the lumbermen played in the Great War.

As the war dragged on into late 1915, the British army realized that it could not supply its men and animals with enough wood to construct the stables, barracks, hospitals and trench works that were needed. In February 1916, the British government requested the Dominion of Canada ship over skilled troops and machinery to assist in the effort to provide milled lumber and timber. The Dominion of Canada acted rapidly on this request and recruited 1,600 men to fill the bill in addition to sending the necessary

Trench with wooden supports. *Author's collection.*

equipment (spending $250,000 in the process). After a quick organization and indoctrination period, the first contingent of the 224th Canadian Forestry Battalion was sent forth and began producing its first sawn lumber on May 13, 1916. Three additional battalions were formed, sent and soon broken down into companies for easier administration, as these units were widely separated throughout England and Scotland. Approximately 22,000 foresters were sent overseas with attached personnel adding an additional 9,000 to the mix. By the war's end, they had produced an astonishing 814 million board feet of sawn wood and an additional 1,114,000 tons of other wood products. Most importantly, their presence, like that of their American counterparts who were soon to be organized, freed up a tremendous amount of shipping space for other necessary military needs, like shells, food and replacement troops.

Nova Scotia provided some of the first recruits for the Canadian contingent, totaling some 525 men. In the process, three companies were organized from the province and neighboring Prince Edward Island. The headquarters of the forestry corps was in Smith's Lawn, Sunningdale and Berkshire in the midst of the Windsor Great Park, formerly the hunting grounds for the royal family. Allegedly, one of the trees harvested for the war effort was the "William the Conqueror Oak," which was said to have measured thirty-eight feet in circumference and was over one thousand years old. Tiny (in population) Newfoundland also sent a contingent of over 500 men who cleared more than 1,200 acres of Scottish timber. One of the "benefits" of recruiting these men was that few needed to worry about rigid physical standards. As a noncombatant unit, the recruiters were able to waive some of these and accept many able-bodied men of minimum age and height for service, and as Governor Sir Walter Davidson wrote, "no one shall be rejected for eyesight, flat feet, loss of fingers, deafness, etc." Many Canadians who would have otherwise been ineligible for military duty were allowed to serve in the forestry units, thus adding their manpower to the effort and providing needed materials to the front line troops in their supporting roles. According to historian Michael O'Hagan, "In all, Canadian foresters produced seventy per cent of the timber used by the Western Allies." It was a grand accomplishment for Canada's forces in addition to its superb fighting divisions. It also represented a severe loss of British forests, with over 450,000 acres cut down. In the postwar era, a new age of British forestry was entered just to replace the lost trees and reinvigorate the land. Americans learned many lessons in modern forestry from their British and French allies.

General John J. "Black Jack" Pershing was not in France long before he realized there was an urgent need for skilled lumbermen; they were needed build the necessary facilities to house, care for and protect American troops. France could not provide the men needed for this task since it had been "bled white" by the latest German offensives and the disastrous Nivelle Offensive of 1917. The "normal" conditions that were seen by the American forces were summed up by Major Edward Hartwick during his tour to inspect one of his companies:

I am sure if you had been with me, you would have pitied and yet admired the fortitude of this French womanhood. The roughest and hardest kind of work, no men to do it. Girls of fourteen, bare headed and bare hands, repairing the road in a snowstorm. Others at work, chopping wood and driving oxen; old women bent and worn, and boys from seven to fifteen, but no able-bodied men, only old men from the front invalided. Women on the railroads—section gangs.

There is no doubt that similar scenes were visited by Pershing when he made his request for the trained foresters of the United States to come over and join the effort to supply the front lines with lumber. Although Pershing was not the first observer to make a call for U.S. foresters, he was the most forceful and important. Major General G.T.M. Bridges, a member of the Balfour Mission in April 1917, had previously asked the war department for such assistance, and on this request, the Tenth Engineers (Forestry) Division was created. The U.S. Forest Service was immediately called on to help form this regiment, and the plan of its organization had been worked out by May 1, 1917. Major James A. Woodruff of the corps of engineers was designated regimental commander and assisted by Captain Beverly C. Dunn; later, Captain Arthur Ringland was named as the adjutant. They, along with other officers and some of the first contingents, set up camp on the grounds of American University in Washington, D.C.

By August 1, 1917, the Tenth Regiment of Engineers had been moved to the American University campground and organized into six companies of 164 men each, not including officers. After some quick and intense training and indoctrination into military life and routine, the regiment was marched out on September 9, 1917, and the following day, they arrived in Hoboken, New Jersey, where they were quickly shuttled to the *Carpathia* for its voyage to Europe. The voyage, in convoy, was relatively uneventful, except for one casualty, Private James Turpin of Clayton, Georgia, who died of spinal meningitis. He was the first of many members to come down with this deadly disease, and by the time the regiment landed at Southhampton, 150 members of the regiment had been placed in quarantine. They finally reached Le Havre, France, on October 7, 1917, part of the first 50,000 American troops to reach France. They were welcomed by typical French fall weather—rain—and were transported in the infamous forty-and-eights (forty men or eight horses) to their first camp in Nevers, France, where they began erecting a temporary camp of pup tents that they lived in for the first week. There, they became acquainted for the first time "with French people, French ways and the notorious French

Forty and eight: railroad cars carrying either forty men or eight horses. *Author's collection.*

mud." The Capathians, as the regiment came to be known, had their first introductions to the French climate in which they labored for much of the remaining war—it was not the French Riviera.

A second and larger unit was needed to supply the forces in the trenches; thus, the Twentieth Engineers (Forestry), the "world's largest regiment," was created. The commanding officer of this regaled regiment was Colonel W.A. Mitchell, a Georgia native and regular army officer who graduated with first honors at West Point. He was ably assisted by Major Edwin E. Hartwick, a prominent Detroit lumberman and the first vice-president of the Guarantee Trust Company of Detroit. Hartwick was the commanding officer of the First Battalion, while Major S.O. Johnson commanded the Second Battalion. Major Johnson was the vice-president of the Weed Lumber Company of Weed, California. Men and officers came from all over the United States, and two of Hartwick's command, Lieutenant R.L. Chaffin of West Palm Beach, Florida, and Lieutenant J.C. Wiliams Jr., the general manager of the Geneva Lumber Company in Eleanor, Florida, represented the Sunshine State in the officer corps. Like the Tenth Regiment before them, the Twentieth Regiment of Engineers commenced their training at the American University camp. The complete unit comprised over 17,000 men in the beginning but grew to well over 18,350 men, including support services.

Even before any forestry units were sent to France, they were preceded by United States forester Henry S. Graves, who was later promoted to lieutenant colonel in November 1917. He was the director of the division of forestry in the American Expeditionary Force (AEF) and was assigned to work out supply problems with the French concerning the purchase and transportation of lumber products needed by the military. Graves also had to work out the future use and need for forestry products for the U.S. forces in France. He was not assigned to any particular unit but reported to Pershing's headquarters directly. Major William B. Greeley was assigned as the deputy director of the headquarters division of forestry for the AEF. He had the monumental task of supervising all lumber operations in France for the AEF. The need for positive and productive supervision was left in the capable hands of these commanders, and like the men under their command, they performed very well under great pressure. With the Tenth and Twentieth Divisions in place, America's lumbermen could begin the monumental task of producing the wood products needed by the men at the front.

The Twentieth Regiment was also unique in that it was one of the few units to lose men to the German submarine offensive. On February 5, 1918, while carrying over two thousand American troops from Hoboken to Liverpool, the SS *Tuscania* was struck by a torpedo fired from UB-77 at around 6:40 p.m. The ship was traveling between Scotland's Islay Isle and Ireland's Rathlin Island, about seven miles north of the Rathlin Lighthouse. This was known as the North Channel route into Liverpool and was taken frequently by troop carriers. The *Tuscania* was a passenger liner of the Anchor Line in peacetime and ran the route between Glasgow and New York. It was the sister ship of the *Transylvania* and had recently been refitted and converted into a troop transport in Glasgow in 1916. It had made a number of successful voyages prior to its encounter with UB-77. In its final voyage, it was part of a convoy of fourteen ships that was set to meet its destroyer escort north of the North Channel entrance. The HX-20 convoy of eight British destroyers was met at the rendezvous point and sailed into the North Channel. Exactly how UB-77 got past the convoy vessels is unknown, but it was there, and Captain Wilhelm Meyer did not lose the chance to take out the transport. Firing two torpedoes at the *Tuscania*, the first missed, but the second struck it just past midship.

The crew and troops acted calmly throughout the ordeal, and three of the destroyers immediately answered the call for help. The ship had shot three red distress rockets into the air, signaling the presence of a U-boat in the area, but that did not deter the men of the three destroyers, the HMS *Grasshopper*, *Mosquito* and *Pigeon*, who bravely went about saving as many as possible. In the growing mist and fog of the early evening, three of the lifeboats filled with military passengers were missed and wound up crashing into the rocks below Islay. More than 50 of the casualties of this tragedy were killed in this accident. By 10:00 p.m., the *Tuscania* had sunk below the waves, taking with it about 150 men. The Twentieth Engineers loss 95 men in this act of war (sources differ on the exact number). These brave men, part of the more than 200 casualties from the ship's sinking, are remembered today by a tower that was erected on the tip of the Oa Peninsula on Islay. The tower is also a reminder of an additional tragedy, the sinking of the line *Otranto*, which occurred in the same waters and took the lives of 470 men, including 357 Americans. This tragedy was the result of a collision between the *Otranto* and HMS *Kashmir* on October 6, 1918. No passage was totally safe in those perilous times.

On the American advance team's arrival in Europe, it became obvious that there was not enough timber on hand to meet the needs of the American forces that were soon to arrive. Colonel James A. Woodruff (who had been newly promoted) wrote to the French minister of armaments

Motor Transport Company, Camp Joseph E. Johnston. *Courtesy of the Florida Memory Project.*

that the United States would have to purchase wood in France; he wrote it was necessary to cancel all shipments of same because of the shortage of ship tonnage to transport wood from the United States. The needs of the American forces were specific and immediate. Primarily, the French ports that were to handle the American forces were not large enough to handle the influx. Since the submarines had forced the convoy system on the Allies, means had to be found that could handle the ten to fifteen ships that would arrive at these ports all at once. There was a need to greatly increase the size of the docks, wharves and storage facilities. Pilings and wharf timbers were required as soon as possible, and lumber for the warehouses, barracks, hospitals and training facilities was also quickly to be supplied. Roads had to be constructed to ship the troops to the front lines, and railroads had to be built to accommodate the supplies, arms and other equipment needed. Because most of the heavy transportation of artillery, hospital wagons and camp equipment was still being done by horses, wood was needed to build the corrals, stables and feed bins for these animals. Fuel wood for warmth and cooking was also needed in vast quantities, and all of this wood had to come from the French forests nearby. By the end of the war, over 650,000 cords of wood had been harvested for American troops' fuel alone. There seemed to be no end to the need of wood for the U.S. Army in France.

In his short but telling piece, "All Wooden on the Western Front," historian Frank N. Schubert noted that one of the first items of business for the forestry regiments was the creation of over two hundred thousand entanglement stakes for the front-line positions. These were the stakes that held up the barbed wire that prevented enemies from entering the trenches. The trenches themselves, as noted earlier, needed wood for the revetments, which were normally composed of planking or bundles of sticks in fascine fashion. These are obvious in the movie *1917*. Importantly, dugouts were constructed of heavy timbers, which Schubert noted the engineers put into four categories based on their ability to withstand enemy fire. Good planking that was covered with corrugated iron and about a foot of earth could withstand most shrapnel shells and protect occupants. Stronger timbers needed an additional four feet of earth to withstand the three-inch (75-mm) shells. For maximum protection, concrete shelters (bunkers) were recommended, and no wood was required to build them. These bunkers protected against the "Jack Johnson" heavy shells that were used by some of the German batteries. Often, troops would place sharply pointed sticks in the ground directly in front of their posts, which would discourage some of the trench raids that both sides practiced throughout the war.

Because of the marl-type soil in Northern France and Belgium, one of the most important uses of wood in the trenches was the construction of "duckboard," which kept the soldiers' feet out of the ever-present water and mud. Schubert quoted one army doctor who proclaimed duckboard as the greatest medical advancement of the war. The English often referred to their version of these devices as "trench mats" because the wood overlapped pieces of board strung together, like a pallet, keeping less mud from oozing through or around the boards.

Temporary hospitals and receiving stations also used large amounts of wood to protect their doctors, nurses, ambulance drivers and patients. So often were these stations and the base hospitals requesting facilities that American engineers came up with the concept of prefabricating these shelters. The twenty-foot-eight-inch frames were shipped along with roof and wall sections, complete with sills, spreaders, bolts, nails and tar paper. These could also be used in the construction of more permanent buildings farther behind the lines.

The need for wood products was never-ending in the war, and its use in railroads was no exception. At least 4 million railroad ties were cut and

Transport lines from storage depots to the front lines. *Author's collection.*

delivered by the foresters in the course of their service. They constructed over 937 miles of standard-gauge railroad tracks in France and a number of unknown narrow-gauge railroad tracks to the front lines. Some of the ties undoubtedly ended up in the roads themselves, as these were frequently shelled and cratered by enemy shelling. Old-fashioned corduroy roads often made do for heavy traffic as long as the horses did not need to cross them (unless they were covered with planking). Finally, as the Germans retreated or as Allied shelling became more accurate, the bridges over rivers, gorges and deep streams were destroyed and had to be repaired before the army could advance. According to one source, over 1.5 million board feet of timber were used just for this function by the

German trenches supported by large tree trunks. *Author's collection.*

Americans alone during the war. If one were to multiply this late-war figure by the number of armies that took the field in all the battlefronts and added three years' worth of fighting, the numbers would be beyond staggering.

One of the more interesting and sometimes confusing facets of the forestry units in France is how they acquired forest land to harvest usable timber. As explained by Percival Ridsdale, the editor of *American Forestry Magazine* in the postwar era:

> *An American officer assigned to forest acquisition work in a given region would look around for forest tracts suitable in character and accessibility for American operations. He would report the suitable tracts to the French officer having charge of forest work in the region. The French officer, after making sure that there was no sufficient reason why the Americans should not have the timber in question, would estimate the amount, appraise the value and mark the timber for cutting. If the owner was satisfied to sell the timber at a reasonable price, his figure would be accepted, but if the owner asked an exorbitant price, the French officer would fix a reasonable price at which the timber would be requisitioned. The French government purchased*

the timber and resold it to the American Army at cost. Rights of way were
obtained in much the same fashion.

The French would often drive a hard bargain, even in the middle of the war, but usually, the Americans got what they needed. The price of the timber was, to American thinking, astonishing. What went for anywhere between two and ten dollars per thousand feet (on the stump) went for anywhere between twenty and forty dollars per thousand feet in Landes, one of the prime areas of French forests. Part of the American surprise was embedded in the fact that American forestry, at that stage of development, was still of the mentality that the forests were inexhaustible, as they appeared that way in the United States. France, on the other hand, had been managing forests for over one hundred years, and their practice was strictly controlled. As noted by Colonel William Greeley: "The French…regard us as wasteful in our use of wood and doubtless think that if they hold us down hard, we can get on with much less than we are asking for. Also, they are taking no chances on exhausting their forests and being put to it for an adequate supply of wood after the war." Luckily, even though many frustrations were experienced by the American forestry regiments, they did have an ally of sorts in Major General Chevalier, the former head of French Engineers and, at the time, the head of the wood supply for the Ministre de Armement. His agreeable nature and ability to persuade his colleagues concerning American needs allowed for some greater flexibility in the allotments of lumber. He even agreed, in the case of an emergency, to allow some cutting in private forests if it were approved by the Comité Interallié de Bois de Guerre. General Chevalier's compromising attitude and ability to negotiate with sometimes difficult French bureaucrats allowed the Americans to get what they needed—even if it was not always on time. It should also be noted that the payment for the wood and right of ways was a form of indirect subsidy to the French in their time of need. It also allowed cash to flow more freely than had been the custom in wartime France.

The lumber industry in America did not greatly benefit from the war in Europe, unlike many other businesses. Indeed, the American lumber industry had not fared well in the years preceding the war. Part of the reason for this was the attitude of Americans regarding their forest heritage. As stated earlier, it was still in the frontier mode to think of the forests as inexhaustible, and therefore, there was little in the way of reforestation or other techniques for revitalizing over-cut land. Florida's forests were treated no differently, and indeed, the state and federal lands were frequently

Bridge to France.
Author's collection.

"raided" by illegal operations, so much so that laws were passed to halt some of the more wasteful practices. One of the more obvious misuses of the forest came when individuals could buy state lands with only a third of the estimated value as a down payment. The purchaser could then clear-cut the valuable timber, sell it and declare that they no longer wanted the land and walk away without paying the other two-thirds of the land's value. Sheriffs and other officers of the law were asked to enforce the laws governing the forests and other state lands, but this was seldom done because of a lack of incentive and the problem of finding personnel to assist them. Forest resources throughout the Southeast, including in Florida, were continually wasted or left undeveloped.

Florida, along with other states in the South, did not produce the new steel ships and vessels that were in vogue at the time of the war. The wooden boat era had pretty much become a thing of the past, except for pleasure crafts and barges; this was also true of the nation's shipbuilding in general.

At the time of the war, the U.S. Merchant Marine was in terrible shape. Although many had seen that the era of the wooden ships had ended with the American Civil War, the shipbuilding industry in America strongly opposed the construction of steel-hulled ships. As a result, according to Christopher J. McMahon, "Many U.S.-flag shipping companies went out of business." More and more American shipping firms used foreign-owned bottoms to ship their goods to overseas markets. Even with the great attention to the modern navy envisioned by Alfred Mahan, the merchant marine was allowed to continue languishing. The Spanish-American War should have been a wake-up call to the country to do something about this deficit in the merchant marine. The Boer War, when Great Britain requisitioned much of the British merchant marine corps to carry troops and arms to South Africa, also should have been a clarion call; however, with all the goods sitting on the docks in the United States and perishable goods rotting on the wharves, little to no action was taken to correct the problem. Even Roosevelt's "Great White Fleet" had to charter foreign-owned vessels to resupply it on that memorable voyage.

At the beginning of World War I, that scene from the Boer War replayed itself, and the American economy suffered greatly due to the lack of commercial shipping. This embarrassing lack of preparedness in commercial shipping facilities finally led to the passage of the Shipping Act of 1916. This act created the U.S. Shipping Board, which was specifically designed to promote and assist the merchant marine. When the United States entered World War I, the board requisitioned the entire U.S. Merchant Marine Corps. Later that same year, 1917, the shipping board initiated a vast shipbuilding program through the creation of the Emergency Fleet Corporation. The shipping board, through the EFC, was contracted for over 1,700 vessels of all types, steel, wood and concrete. Combined with the ships planned for in the Naval Act of 1916, the total number of vessels to be constructed was closer to 2,851 commercial vessels, 156 warships and other additional tonnage. The southeastern United States had the timber, manpower and desire, but it did not have shipyards large enough to fit the bill. When the board decided to build more wooden boats, things began to look up for Florida and the other states of the Southeast.

The EFC's call for wooden ships (many of the Ferris design) led to a rapid increase in shipyard construction. When the call came out in 1917, there were a reported 51 shipyards building wooden vessels. By September 1, 1918, there were 131 shipyards producing wooden vessels. Florida benefited from this boom in wooden ship building as a number of firms spread throughout the state. Jacksonville benefited more than most other places in the Southeast, as the Hillyer-Sperring-Dunn Company (later the St. Johns River S.B. Company) got the largest contracts. Also located in the Jacksonville area were the Morey & Thomas Company and the J.W. Murdock Company. The Tampa Dock Company received the contract to build five Ferris-type boats and other smaller vessels, including a barge. The American Lumber Company of Millville (near Panama City) received a contract for eight barges. The American Lumber Company was formerly the German American Lumber Company with headquarters in Pensacola and a facility in Millville. Pensacola's Fore River received a contract to construct a steel-hulled vessel of an unknown style. Tampa's Merrill-Stevens Yard also received a contract, but this contract was canceled because the war had ended by that time.

Indeed, many of the contracted vessels were never constructed or became mothballed because of the war's end. Nationally, of the over 1,700 contracted ships, only 107 were delivered prior to the war's end. What had promised to be the beginning of a new, viable industry for Florida and the Southeast fizzled before it could boom. Unfortunately, the national government learned nothing from this or its previous history with the merchant marine. In the two decades following World War I, the American Merchant Marine again became mired in neglect and continued to decline until World War II appeared on the horizon. With the passage of the Merchant Marine Act of 1936, things began to turn around—and just in time.

The only other immediate demand for timber came from the fledgling aircraft industry. Although Florida had a large role in the growth of that industry, it was mostly on the consumer side of the ledger. During the First World War, Florida was a base for training hundreds of pilots and was home to numerous air bases, but it did not have any appreciable impact on the construction of aircraft. The largest reason for this was the fact that most of the early wooden planes were constructed of northwest spruce, a wood pliable and light enough to fill the need.

Without a doubt, the forestry industry has a lot to be proud of with its contribution to the American effort in World War I. Over 4 million railroad ties kept the French roads running back and forth to the front with materials and men, setting the bar high for any evaluation. The construction and development of Brest, Saint-Nazaire and other ports in France greatly helped the recovery of that war-torn country in addition to the facilities they left behind, including warehouses, docks and wharves, machinery and deeper port facilities via the dredging done by the U.S. Army Corps

"Building a pontoon bridge." *Literary Digest,* September 1, 1918. *Author's collection.*

of Engineers. Given the fact that the foresters produced over 220 million board feet of lumber as well as the railroad ties, bridge pilings, entanglement stakes and bundles of wood for fuel and trench construction shows that this was a pivotal group in the war effort of the United States. Its no wonder that Colonel William Parsons of the Eleventh Engineers (Railroad) would proclaim that lumber was, indeed, a major munition of war. A more fitting tribute could hardly be found.

5

AERIAL PHOTOGRAPHIC RECONNAISSANCE IN WORLD WAR I AND ITS IMPACT ON THE DEVELOPMENT OF FLORIDA

Nearly everyone is familiar with the stories of antiquity, like that of Elias who ascended to the heavens in his fiery chariot, never to be seen on earth again; or the tale of Icarus who disregarded his father's advice and flew too close to the sun and lost his wings, falling tragically into the sea. And, of course, we have all shared a laugh at the expense of those wonderful "flapping, flying" men who failed to fly and fell back to earth, usually dying or being severely injured. Some of the contraptions invented over the decades to attempt heavier-than-air flight also have provoked laughter and glee. It was not until the development of balloons that were capable of carrying man aloft that people could actually envision the possibilities of aerial photography. Of course, photographic equipment capable of taking pictures also needed to be invented before a marriage of the two inventions could lead to a revolution in military affairs.

One of the most notable ascensions in a balloon came with the flight of Jean-Pierre Blanchard and John Jefferies, a Tory doctor who waited out the American Revolution in England. The pair took off from Dover on January 7, 1785, and hopped, skipped and flew over the waves, crashing in France about twelve miles inland from Calais; Blanchard, sans pantaloons and other nonessential equipment, made a relatively safe landing. It was a fantastic feat but also had other implications in addition to proving that flight was a possibility. It proved that the insulated island of England was no longer so isolated as to be immune from attack, as the German Zeppelins

Military balloon ascent.
Author's collection.

exemplified in World War I. Interest in flight increased in England and elsewhere, including in the United States, where a number of Frenchmen and Americans willingly tried their hands at ballooning. One of the more successful aviators was one Guille, who, in 1819, made a flight over Jersey City and then parachuted five hundred feet safely to ground, the first such jump in American history.

After a number of other experiments in France and the United States, the first attempts to take a photograph from the air, primarily from kites, resulted in images that were, as imagined, not sharp. Yes, Louis M. Daguerre did invent the daguerreotype, but it took a dark area to develop these images, which made it difficult to send his invention aloft for creating aerial prints. The first aerial photographs belonged to one Gaspard-Félix Tournachon, popularly known as "Nadar," in 1858. These were taken from a tethered balloon at a height of eighty meters. None of the originals of this group survive today, but those taken of Paris in 1868 do. During the Civil War in the United States, some aerial photographs were allegedly taken by Thaddeus Lowe, but there is no evidence that such an event was recorded.

Maps made from drawings of the observers in these balloons were much more accurate than those done on the ground under fire from the enemy and were important in a number of engagements. Maps made from photographs taken from kites emerged in 1882, when English meteorologist E.D. Archibald successfully sent up a string of kites with the camera attached to the last one. Even rockets got into the act early on with the 1906 Albert Maul launching of a compressed air rocket, which reached the height of 2,600 feet and took a photograph with a camera (newly invented by George Eastman in 1899 with nitro-cellulose film) that was ejected from the rocket and parachuted to earth. Of course, small cameras were already being developed that could fit on a carrier pigeon, as demonstrated by the Bavarian Pigeon Corps in 1903.

There were other firsts in the history of aerial photography in this era; the most important was that of the 1909 aerial image that was taken by Wilbur Wright using a motion picture camera above Centocelle, Italy. It was soon obvious that the art of aerial photography would play a major role in the oncoming war in 1914.

While all these developments were taking place, Florida experienced its first aircraft when Lincoln Beachey flew a motorized airship over Jacksonville in 1908. As one of the first graduates of the Curtiss School, he was also considered one of its most able. Two short years later, in February 1910, he flew the first heavier-than-air ships over Orlando. Beachey was a popular young man with a quiet, amiable appearance. Although he was a showman in the air, he was relatively modest in his public appearances. His instructor in flight at the Curtiss School was Jack D. McCurdy, who, in 1911, attempted to fly from Key West to Havana but came up a little short. Luckily, the other contestants in the race did not make it as far. Not to be frightened by this attempt, McCurdy ordered another Curtiss biplane in Cuba and made the return trip. Later that same year, he was involved in a new experiment, using a Marconi wireless receiver (assisted by Percy Morriss, a Marconi wireless engineer) to receive messages from passing ships and points as far away as Key West. This is believed to have been the first such use of a radio in aviation. (Messages had been sent via wire using Morse code during the Civil War.) A month later, in March 1911, Beachey flew a night flight over Tampa, the first such flight in the Sunshine State. Another pilot familiar to later Floridians, Johnnie Greene, had completed a night flight over Knoxville, Tennessee, in June 1910. Meanwhile, as Florida enjoyed the novelty of flight, Italian captain Carlo Piazza was flying his machine over Turkish gun emplacements but had difficulty recording all that he saw. He requested a camera be mounted on the belly of his plane, a Bleriot aircraft, and he reconnoitered the Turkish positions again. While not clear, the results were good enough to make a limited beginning in aerial photography for military purposes.

The year 1911 was innovative for the fledgling U.S. Army Air Service (as it was then called). A young lieutenant by the name of Benjamin D. Foulois, who, in 1909, had flown as the observer in Wilbur Wright's flight to get the army contract for the further development of their airplanes, met Frank L. Perry, the Chicago-based ham radio operator, and collaborated on the creation of ground-to-cockpit receivers. By hooking up antennas to the plane, the two were able to install a battery-operated receiver behind the pilot's seat. At the fifth-annual Electric Show in Chicago in January 1910, they tried their experiment out and were successful in transmitting a message from the ground to the plane, the first in the United States. Foulois, not one to take no for an answer, then applied to the army to try out his device during the regular military exercises along the Rio Grande River in 1911. He finally received permission and took off with his Wright-trained pilot, Philip O. Parmelee, and they scouted along the river for the "enemy" troops. The flight was 106 miles in length and was flown at 1,200 feet. No enemies were spotted. The next flights had another passenger, a photographer from *Collier's* magazine, who took a number of pictures of the terrain and established the possibility that aerial photography could be very useful for military operations. Five years later, Foulois and others were actually doing this in the exasperating hunt for Pancho Villa. In that campaign, the First Aero Squadron, under Foulois, did its part in photographing the landscape and relaying messages and scouting for the Pershing-led expedition. Toward the end of the American involvement in this affair, the squadron acquired more and better planes and the newer Brock automatic cameras that took pictures continuously along the paths of the planes. Foulois's men experimented with enlarging the prints and transferring the results to maps for the benefit of the troops on the ground. It was good and necessary training for the immediate future in Europe. This was especially true for the planes used by the squadron, none of which survived the expedition intact. "The deficient, unsuitable airplanes the 1st Aero Squadron took to Mexico also served as a warning for the future." The U.S. military did not fly any American-manufactured planes during World War I, and those that did make it to Europe were mostly trainers.

The main problem for American forces entering the war was the lack of weapons, planes, vehicles, medical supplies and personnel and almost everything involved in going to war. The Wilson administration had resisted any attempts to prepare for war and spent very little on military supplies or training. During the Mexican crisis, Foulois tried to increase the budget for planes and spare parts, but the bureaucrats in Washington refused the simple requests. The main culprit was the new head of the section and non-flyer William "Billy" Mitchell. World War I changed everything for the flyers and their squadrons. The "Kahn Committee" in Congress, at France's request (Ribot), increased the funding immediately. Part of the evidence was that Germany entered the war with nearly 1,000 airplanes, France mustered about 300 and England another 250. America had fewer than 100, and most were obsolete. The United States had done little to encourage manufacturers to supply more modern planes, and of the almost twelve firms making planes, only half could make them to government specifications. Of the 59 ready to go at the beginning of the United States' entry into the war, 4 were made by different firms, and their parts were not interchangeable. Major Raynal C. Bolling was sent to Europe to see what the Allies had and needed from the United States. The Bolling Commission's report was a revelation, and Congress reacted with the passage of an act appropriating $640 million.

One of the big problems for American-made airplanes was their lack of power, and the United States would not buy the Rolls-Royce. Instead, it asked the Packard Corporation to come up with something more affordable. Using the Vincent Hall idea of interchangeable cylinders for all engines, the company came up with the "Liberty engine," one of the few industrial successes of the war. Although a large number of Liberty engines did find their way to the Allies, American-made aircraft did not.

Another area of concern to Foulois and the fledgling service was spare parts and materials. Making an airplane for the air service required 500 to 1,000 feet of lumber of the right kind (mostly spruce) to withstand the stress of flight. Most planes were covered with fabric at this stage of the production, and the flax for this came from Ireland (it took 250 to 500 yards of material to cover the craft). At that time, Ireland was under the German submarine net, and most of its product was sold in advance to the Allies. Training mechanics to repair and maintain the planes was another major problem, and special schools had to be set up to produce the number needed (they never did during the war). An Air Service Mechanics Department was established in August 1917 and was immediately divided into two courses, an "airplane" course headed by Captain D.J. Neumuller and an "aero motors" course headed by Captain Vernon Burge, a seasoned mechanic and pilot. There were only five major schools to teach new corps members how to fly; one of these schools was Carlstrom Field in Arcadia, Florida. The mechanics school was charged with producing 2,500 mechanics a month, a totally unrealistic number. The classrooms were simply tents constructed about a mile from the base at Kelly Field in Texas. There was a constant struggle with unit commanders who needed planes in the air and were under constant pressure to get machines flying. The result was erratic attendance in classes and little continuity in instruction. The final insult to the mechanics' school came at Christmastime in 1917, when a storm blew down the instruction tents and scattered the materials over the base. The school was soon transferred to the new Rich Field outside of Waco, Texas.

Open house at Dorr Field in Arcadia, Florida.
Courtesy of the Manatee County Public Library.

While all of this national action was taking place, predominantly rural Florida was experiencing something new. The city of St. Petersburg, a city of nearly nine thousand in 1912, was trying to make more headway with rival Tampa across the bay. The only way tourists and potential settlers could reach the city was by taking a long road around the top of the Pinellas Peninsula or via boat. The railroad that had been constructed by Peter Demens and backed by Hamilton Disston and others was nearly just a memory. The old Orange Belt Railroad had been absorbed by the Atlantic Coast Line Railroad, and its line left many a little short of their destinations. The only spur ran to Indian Rocks Beach, but when the two main hotels of that lovely expanse burned down in 1912, the spur was abandoned. St. Petersburg and Pinellas County were looking for an alternative form of transportation. As things were heating up in Europe, Percival Fansler, a sales representative for Kahlenberg Brothers and maker of marine diesel engines, became interested in the racing ventures of Anthony H. Jannus, who had recently flown a flying boat built by Tom Benoist of St. Louis, Missouri, down the Mississippi River. Fansler and Benoist corresponded and hatched the idea of connecting St. Petersburg with Tampa by flying boat, creating publicity and profit from carrying a few passengers and the mail. With the enthusiastic support of the St. Petersburg business community, the first regularly scheduled airline connecting the two cities began business on January 1, 1914. It was a national event, as this was the first commercial airline in North America. Tony Jannus was hired to be the first pilot. Others, including Curtiss, soon followed to train Johnnie Greene.

Miami was not out of the picture in early Florida flights. The city wrote to Wright Brothers to ask the company to send one of its planes and a pilot down to Miami for the fifteenth anniversary of the city's founding. Everest G. Sewell headed the committee and was an early booster of the "Magic City." For a fee of $7,500, Wright Brothers agreed to send down, by train, one of its planes and a "birdman" (pilot) to make three flights on July 20 and three more on July 21. Miami became infected with a new disease, "aeroplanitis," of which one of the main symptoms was a straining of the neck. The Miami Golf Links was to be the site of the new demonstration of air power. The field was crowded with residents and visitors from afar, waiting for the first south Florida flight. When Howard Gill, the aviator, appeared, the band played, the crowds cheered and the little wooden, cloth-covered biplane was wheeled out by two attendants. The thirty-five-horsepower engine roared to life as Gill took control. The little plane ran down the makeshift runway and then ascended. After circling the field at just above treetop level a few times, the plane came back to rest. The crowd roared its approval, and two more short flights followed. On the following day, Gill took to the sky and ascended to the height of 7,500 feet, becoming a mere speck in the sky. Then the motor "died," and the crowd hushed. Were they about to see a deadly crash? After plummeting much of the distance toward the earth, Gill leveled the plane off, and the motor roared again. The crowd took a deep, grateful breath and exhaled in unison. In less than a year, Glenn Curtiss introduced his hydroplane to Miami and met with Sewell to arrange the opening of a new school for pilots in South Florida. Charles C. Witmer, an experienced Curtiss pilot, was selected to run the new school. Aviation then had roots in Florida that could not be denied.

The navy had gotten into the act early concerning flying but had done little to expand it. With the situation heating up in Europe, the navy decided to reactivate the old Pensacola Naval Station, and it had a skeleton crew there when the war began. The site was chosen unanimously by the board, which was set up with Captain Washington Irving Chambers as its head. The first complement of airplanes was anchored by six Curtiss, one Wright and two Burgess seaplanes. On February 1, 1914, the first airman died when Lieutenant James M. Murray's Burgess crashed while flying a D-1 flying boat. Among the first "graduates" of the flight training was a Quincy, Florida native, Lieutenant Commander W.M. Corry Jr., who died in 1920 while attempting to save another passenger when their plane crashed and burned. By 1915, the station had a few men, a meager organization, and the crews lived in tents. Almost all of the men on duty there were sent individually, not as an organized group. In the summer of 1915, John Towers was given the task of organizing the schooling and given the grandiose title of supervisor of the Naval Reserve Flying Corps. It was not until war had actually been declared that the things began to move rapidly. On April 20, 1917, the first DN-1 made an appearance and flew the first flight at Pensacola. So poorly was this craft made that after two more dismal flights, it was permanently grounded. On May 5, 1917, the navy tested the Curtiss R-3 machine guns, which fired through the propellers while taxiing on the water. The next day, the newly established aircraft production board ended the feud between the Curtiss companies and the Wrights, thus enabling mass production of the airplanes. The Pensacola station also successfully tested the idea of radio transmission from a plane to a land station; it was heard in New Orleans, nearly 140 miles away.

Other naval stations in Florida participated in the development and training of pilots and mechanics. Key West was a busy place during the war and was visited by Thomas Alva Edison, who developed a marine depth charge while there. A seaplane and blimp station were also created on the island. The naval air station at Key West was commissioned on December 18, 1917. Its main purposes were elementary flight training and marine patrol duties, primarily searching for German U-boats. Curtiss's land in Miami also became a busy place. Pilot training was the main objective of the station. Curtiss also donated the land for the first marine aviation training site. Lieutenant Alfred Cunningham took the lead in attempting to get an independent marine aviation section and took part in the negotiations with Curtiss for his land west of downtown Miami, which they eventually leased for a dollar a year. Navy lieutenant Pat Bellinger chose the site of Dinner Key for an Atlantic coast seaplane base. Over 150 seaplanes and between 900 and 1,800 men called the base home. Like the navy and marine pilots in Pensacola, the south Florida flyers trained hard, spotting submarines, bombing and artillery. Florida definitely had a place in the nation's defense plans.

"World War I was, more than any other conflict to that point, a war of maps. Maps were used by the militaries engaged in the war for many purposes: making defensive preparations, planning offensives, training, etc." Perhaps the most important role of the cartographers in the war was to use maps to pinpoint enemy artillery for carrying out strikes against these targets with preregistration fire, which gave away the intentions of the military. Surprise was added again to the arsenal of the military planners. With this important element, the war of movement, so prized by General John J. Pershing, was made possible again. Preregistering targets made the rolling barrage and counter-battery fire more effective, which suppressed the enemy's ability to strike the attacking force. In a war where it is estimated that 60 percent of all casualties were caused by artillery fire (including gas), this was an important and lifesaving element. Much of the accuracy of the artillery fire came from the air reconnaissance units. As Del Kostka has put it recently: "The accuracy and timeliness of the intelligence

Left: A submarine bombed by a plane. *Image from* History's Greatest War: A Pictorial Narrative, *1919.*

Below: A box camera being handed to photographer and gunner in the rear of airplane. *Author's collection.*

they gathered changed the nature of warfare, and the devastating artillery barrages they orchestrated from high above the battlefield accounted for more casualties than any other weapon system of the Great War. Simply put, the reconnaissance aircrew was the most lethal killing machine of World War I." In this lethality, the excellent job of mapping enemy positions and the rapidity of translating aerial photography onto maps that could be used within hours must be included. Timeliness was an important element in the success of these efforts.

Interpreting the photographic intelligence was another matter for all parties. Even the British and French had to learn on the job, and they both found (as did the Germans and Austrians) that although photographic intelligence was useful, most of the equipment left much to be desired. The British Royal Flying Corps began running experiments on new types of equipment and created a provisional unit to assess the progress of these works. Working with the Thornton-Pickard Ltd. Group, the British came up with a box-design camera that was mounted toward the front of the airplane. It was far too cumbersome to be practical, but it did lead to many modifications that continued to be made throughout the course of the war. Since the United States entered the war so late, it relied heavily on the British and French experience to guide its efforts.

In addition to assisting the artillery in its barrages and sending information to the infantry about what lay ahead, the third primary mission of the photographic intelligence forces was to see beyond the enemy lines and look for telltale signs of enemy presence, including new weapons emplacements, presence of smoke, fresh tracks in open fields, amassing of personnel, vehicle traffic and signs of new or differing camouflage techniques. The initial task of photoreconnaissance was to be ancillary to the visual reports; however, as the war progressed and cameras improved, it was important to interpret what was recorded. Imagine leaning out of the cockpit of a two-seater, six to eight thousand feet in the air, temperatures numbing your fingers and the plane jarring the camera around in your hands—it was a nearly impossible task. Fuselage-mounted cameras, which reduced vibration distortion and kept a relatively even keel during the flight, made these tasks easier.

The role of the reconnaissance units became one of the most important jobs for the infant army air service. Men of the talent of Edward Steichen, who rose in the ranks to command one of the photoreconnaissance sections in France, took great pride in the work they did, even when some of the conservative commanding officers initially doubted their worth. Reconnaissance was the selling point for military aviation. It became such

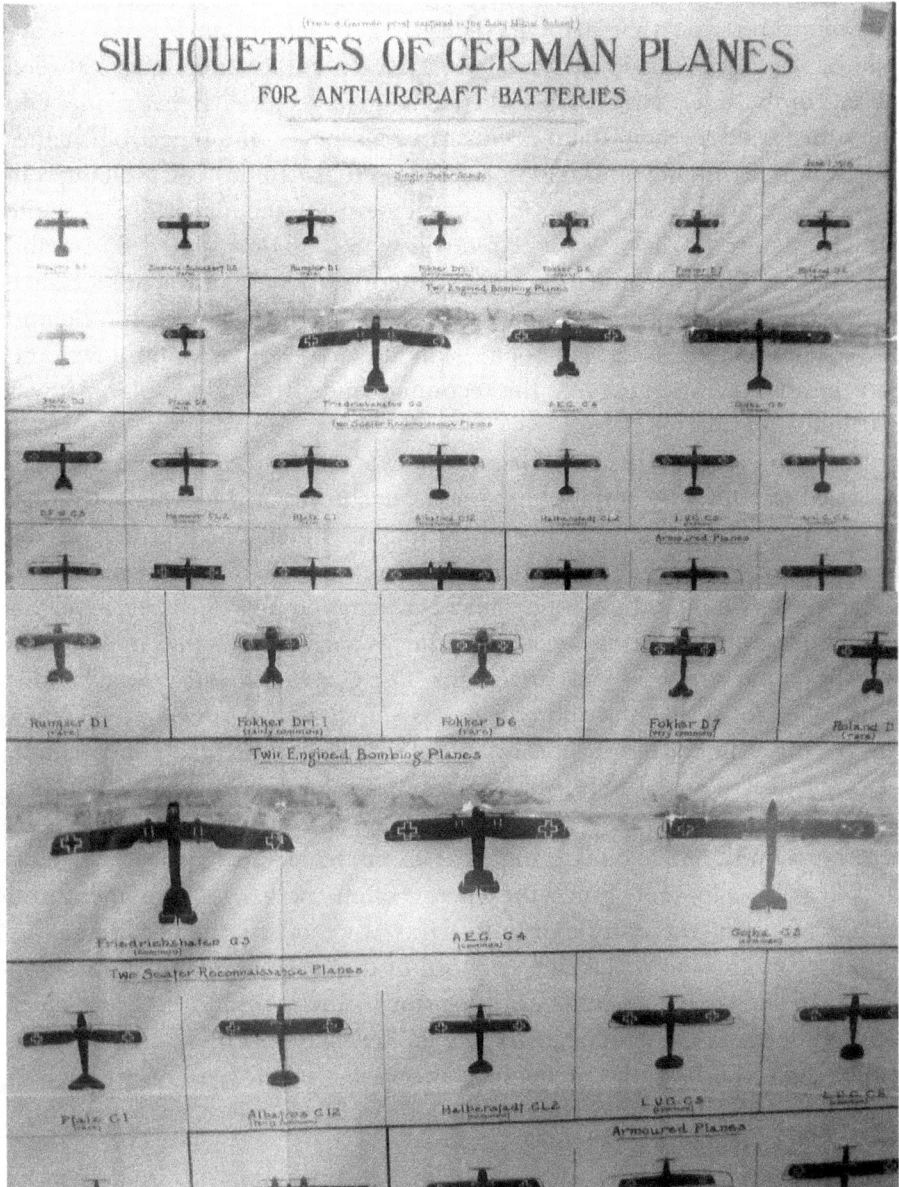

Silhouettes of German planes. *Courtesy of the Janelle Sherouse Collection.*

an important role that armed escorts began accompanying the "scout planes" on their missions. This led to the legendary dogfights between aerial combatants in which one side defended its reconnaissance planes and the other tried to deny them access to its airspace. Bombing from planes was still in its infancy and had not progressed as rapidly as the changes in aerial photography. The most famous elements of the air service were the attack squadrons, those flying daredevils who took on the Red Baron and his cohorts. They became important as escorts to the photoreconnaissance planes, most of which were unarmed. Rising high in the sky, sun behind the defenders and in the face of the enemy, they would swoop down and attack those trying to prevent the reconnaissance from taking place. It was a true team effort.

One of the biggest problems facing the U.S. intelligence officers who were assigned to study the aerial photographs, according to Lieutenant Colonel Marlborough Churchill, the chief of the military intelligence branch, was the lack of readily available aerial photography (other than those contained in the few texts on the subject). The officers assigned to this duty took an eight-week course at the British school at Harrow, which included photograph interpretation as part of the curriculum. The U.S. doctrine developed at this time called for systematic and repeated coverage of the same area to detect any changes in the landscape, shape of the trenches, new construction, et cetera. Of course, there were limitations to photoreconnaissance, such as the presence of enemy aircraft, ground protections (ack-ack fire), poor weather conditions (clouds, rain, dust from troop movements, et cetera) and faulty equipment. Since the enemy often moved its equipment and troops at night, the early-morning flights were often the most revealing. Photoreconnaissance became so important that a great deal of innovation was spawned by its productivity. Just prior to the World War II, the chief of the German General Staff, General Werner von Fritsch stated: "The nation with the best photoreconnaissance will win the war." Anyone who has studied the invasion of Europe of June 6, 1944, will testify to the truth of that statement.

One of the most innovative of the officers assigned to the photographic unit was Major James W. Bagley, who, prior to the war, had worked in the United States Geological Survey (USGS). His specific assignment was to test a three-lens aerial camera. The concept was to use this camera to map terrestrial features so that one would be able to judge depth and contours via stereoscopic lenses. Bagley's team arrived in Europe too late to test the camera under combat conditions, but after the armistice, his team ran test runs over the Meuse-Argonne and Saint-Mihiel battlefields and was found to be an appropriate tool for evaluation. There were some design changes recommended, such as a longer lens focal length, but it was judged to be of value for civilian use. After the war, the Bagley design became a key instrument in civilian aerial photography. A modified Bagley design was used for some of the civilian tasks assigned to the Army Corps of Engineers after the war.

The rapid demobilization of the military after the war left a number of very talented men with training that proved valuable for civilian use. By the end of the war, the U.S. Air Service (AEF) had 195,023 men under its command. By the middle of 1919, the air service had been reduced to 15,875 men. Many wondered what to do with these talented and dedicated men. Not all could be elected to Congress like Hiram Bingham or go to work for a major coal company like James Meissner. Although many joined the reserve units, this was not a full-time employment option. Surveying, engineering and other technical employment opportunities were offered to many who served as mechanics in the air service. Coastal mapping took place along the southern Florida coast and Cuba in 1924. The flyers from the Pensacola Naval Air Station assisted in mapping the channel that was dug by the ACE through Lake Okeechobee, which connected the St. Lucie River Canal to the Caloosahatchee River. The flights took place in April and June 1924, and the aerial photography was shot from six thousand feet. Changes in coastlines due to storms, especially in the 1920s, were mapped almost exclusively from the air, with many private firms, like Dillon Engineers of Fort Lauderdale, participating in this effort. Assessments of damage from the storms and recovery efforts were also aided by aerial photography.

Of course, many of the developers of the great land boom of the 1920s used many aerial photographs in their advertisements. Like most veterans of the war, the men returned home and tried to renew their old positions and habits. Most succeeded in adjusting to civilian life, but many did not. Many who served in Florida or were trained there, like those thousands after the Second World War, found the Sunshine State to be to their liking and remained to become part of one of the greatest land booms in American history. With the skills they learned in the air service, many continued to work in the aviation field or worked to improve the aerial mapping of Florida and the rest of the country. Finally, one of the true benefits for Florida was that it had a growing international connection with South America and the Caribbean. Flights out of Miami to the islands and later to the southern continent became possible in the years following the war and have continued to the present day. Juan Tripp and Pan American Airways, Eddie Rickenbacker and others formed Florida Airlines, and Arthur Burns Chalk started Chalk's International Airlines; all of them got their starts in the greater Miami area, and their legacies live on today. Aviation and Florida just seem to go together and have since World War I.

6

BLOCKADE AND CONVOYS

he U.S. Navy had two main functions in the First World War aside from protecting American shores. Prior to the American entry into the war, it was assumed, based on British reporting, that the naval side of the conflict was well in the hands of the Grand Fleet, which was stationed at Scapa Flow. This was not the case. With the unrestricted submarine warfare taking huge tolls in British and neutral shipping, the Grand Fleet was struggling. Just prior to America's official declaration of war against Germany, the U.S. Navy sent Admiral William Sims to explore an Anglo-American effort to control the submarine menace. What Sims found was shocking to the American naval establishment and the federal government. Sims arrived in Liverpool on April 9, 1917, and was met by Rear Admiral Hope, the envoy on behalf of Admiral John Jellicoe, first sea lord of the admiralty. Sims was handed a letter communicating Jellicoe's pleasure that Sims had been appointed, but it ended with ominous words: "The situation is far from easy, solely on account of the submarine warfare, but difficulties are there to be overcome, and they will be overcome, I am convinced; although I fully expect our losses to be very heavy before all is over." As this letter came from Sims's old friend Jellicoe, he had to wonder what on earth could this mean.

After arriving in London on the following day, Sims met with Jellicoe, who handed him a memorandum after the formal greeting. The memorandum outlined the losses incurred by the British and neutrals in the first quarter of the year; around 1,300,000 tons of shipping had been sunk and nearly

(*Left*) U.S. admiral William Sims. (*Right*) Rear Admiral Henry B. Wilson, commanding American Naval Forces in France. *Author's collection.*

900,000 had been sunk in the month of April. Sims was dumfounded and quizzed his friend. "Yes," replied Jellicoe quietly, "it is impossible for us to go on with the war if losses like this continue." Sims stated boldly that it looked as if the Germans might win the war, to which Jellicoe replied, "They will win, unless we can stop these losses—and stop them soon." When Sims inquired about solutions, Jellicoe replied that they had none at that moment. When other officials attempted to withhold some information concerning these losses, Sims, according to biographer Elting Morison, stated that nothing could be gained by withholding information and that he had to have the facts to properly advise his government. England was desperate, and there was no getting around it.

Sims dutifully reported his dreary findings to Admiral William S. Benson, chief of naval operations, and Secretary of the Navy Josephus Daniels. Sims relayed his concern about the concept of the convoy system to Jellicoe and others and strongly advocated that it be adopted by the Allies. A few smaller convoys had been attempted from Gibraltar to England, and each was successful in not having any losses to submarines, but they were not successful enough to convince Jellicoe and many in the Royal Navy. Sims, on the other hand, had the backing of Secretary Daniels and the president. The opposition to a convoy system, surprisingly, was led by the private sea captains and ship owners. They expressed concern over the slowness of the convoy, which depended on the speed of its slowest member. They also doubted if independently minded sea captains would submit to the discipline required to keep a large number of ships in formation. Some even thought a convoy would present an even more tempting target to a submarine than a single ship in the vast ocean. The exact opposite was actually true, as it was harder to spot a convoy in the vastness of the open ocean than hundreds of single ships in the normal shipping lanes at a particular time. The escorting vessels, normally destroyers, were also deployed to take the offensive against any submarines that happened to be spotted, which acted as a deterrent on many occasions. The slowness issue was resolved by keeping the convoys moving between twelve and fifteen knots, if possible. The speed was important, since submarines, if submerged, rarely reached eleven knots in the open ocean and only about fifteen above the surface, which made them the targets of armed merchants and escorting destroyers. But the basic fact remained: the United States had a number of destroyers available to take up the escort duties and could build more quickly to add to the strength of the convoys.

The results of the convoys spoke for themselves after their first three months of duty. Sims, a strong advocate of the convoys system, had the near-unanimous backing of the American hierarchy but disagreed with Benson's policy of holding back several destroyers for the defense of the East Coast from submarine bombardment or other disruption. The disagreement went away after Benson's mid-1917 visit to the war zone. According to Sims's associate and member of the London planning staff, Captain Dudley W. Knox, "This marked a great turning point in the war, made possible by the naval forces which had become available through America's entry." To make the point clearer, Knox noted that the huge shipping losses of 881,000 tons in April 1917 had been reduced to 289,000 in November 1917. The convoys made the difference.

U.S. secretary of the navy Josephus Daniels. *Author's collection.*

As previously noted, destroyers were the backbone of the convoy system once the whole operation came together. However, battleships also took part in these convoys, at least in northern waters. The sea trade with Scandinavia was important for iron and other metal shipments that provided the metal for the army and navy of the empire. Denmark and Sweden, additionally, were active centers of espionage for the Germans as well as the British. The Baltic fleets were topics of

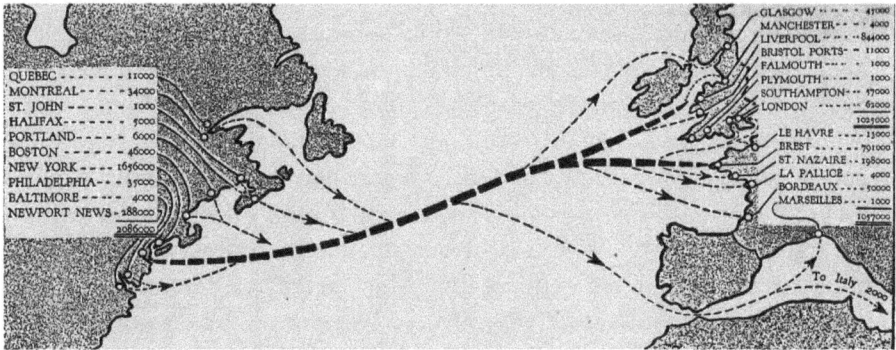

QUEBEC - - - - - 11000
MONTREAL - - - - 34000
ST. JOHN - - - - - 1000
HALIFAX - - - - - 5000
PORTLAND - - - - 6000
BOSTON - - - - - 46000
NEW YORK - - - 1656000
PHILADELPHIA - - 35000
BALTIMORE - - - - 4000
NEWPORT NEWS - 288000
2086000

GLASGOW ·· ·· · 41000
MANCHESTER - · 4000
LIVERPOOL - · · - 844000
BRISTOL PORTS - 11000
FALMOUTH · · 1000
PLYMOUTH · · - 1000
SOUTHAMPTON - · 47000
LONDON · · · - 62000
1025000

LE HAVRE - - - 13000
BREST - - - - - 791000
ST. NAZAIRE - - 198000
LA PALLICE - - - 4000
BORDEAUX - - - 50000
MARSEILLES - - - 1000
1057000

To Italy 4000

Transporting ten thousand men a day. *Author's collection.*

constant gossip, espionage and observation. After the Battles of Dogger Bank and Jutland, the Grand Fleet was on its toes for any movement of the German High Seas Fleet, especially sallies coming out after the Baltic convoys, which served a dual purpose. The primary purpose of the convoys was the delivery of iron, timber and minerals to Britain and its allies, but its secondary purpose was to lure the High Seas Fleet out for a fight to the death, if such were possible. Given the protective attitude of Kaiser Wilhelm II toward his fleet, this was not likely. However, since the two major sea battles of the northern waters, the Grand Fleet was standing guard in case the Germans finally did decide to come out and fight. However, with the addition of the American battleships to the Grand Fleet on December 7, 1917, the Germans were heavily outgunned in a Jutland-like battle scene.

U.S. Battleship Division Nine, commanded by Admiral Hugh Rodman, sailed out of Lynnhaven Roads, Virginia, on November 25, 1917, and arrived at Scapa Flow after fighting a major storm (hurricane) on November 30, which carried away the topmasts of all four battleships, making radio communication impossible. The original four battleships were the *New York*, *Wyoming*, *Delaware* and *Florida*. They were accompanied by the destroyer *Manley*. During the storm, the *Delaware*, *Florida* and *Manley* were driven off course, with only the *Florida* rejoining the flagship. In the words of R.H. Bennett, who served on the *Florida*:

> *There we were, the division separated by a winter gale and en route for the war zone. Of course, there was a small chance that we would encounter a hostile fleet; in fact, we were entering the zone of the British Isles entirely dominated by the British Fleet, an ally. Naturally, the zone was also used by the German submarines en route to Atlantic trade lanes, yet that*

was not a major menace. Nevertheless, we conducted our approach just as if we faced a hostile fleet. The American contingent was immediately designated the Sixth Battle Squadron and given routine instructions, fleet special orders and assigned a signal quartermaster with a number of signalmen until our signal forces learned the British system. And the weather—"perfectly rotten."

By the time minor repairs were made and the men settled into some sort of routine, the troops aboard the *Florida* were placed under quarantine with the mumps.

One thing should be noted: the American fleet, according to the British commanders, did not measure up to British standards, especially regarding shooting accuracy. Since most of the fleet crews were not old hands with the navy, that is not surprising. One of the problems of any start-up project is the lack of trained personnel, and the navy was no different. A couple of the battleships in U.S. fleet were constantly being used as trainers for other vessels. It was a frustrating job for many who longed for fighting on the front lines. As R.H. Bennett noted,

I was tremendously restless. Here was the greatest war in progress the world had ever known, and undoubtedly, I would see nothing of it but this mere preparation. Like so many regular army officers who never got overseas because they had to drill and train at concentration camps, here we were

The *Florida* "In a Heavy Sea." *Author's collection.*

The USS *Florida. Courtesy of Wikipedia.*

> *similarly marooned on battleships, forever at base 2, drilling, training and*
> *holding examinations for men bound for the war zone.*

Another sign of the inexperience of the sailors was the frequent sighting of enemy periscopes, which the officers, both American and British, sluffed off as jitters of the new men. Boredom also plagued the men, who were not used to wartime experience. Bennett spent some of his spare time reading from the ship's library and came across Robert Louis Stevenson's piece on spring in Edinburgh. "He never had been to Scapa Flow," Bennett observed. But even with all the faults of the new crews and assignments, the Americans did advance; they ran very efficient ships and maintained good discipline throughout their stay.

Admiral Hugh Rodman was an excellent choice to work with the British. His fleet-wide reputation as an excellent storyteller, his normally jovial manner and his experience in the navy made him relatively popular among the men. Rodman also realized that his fleet was new to warfare and needed seasoning. Working in the British system was also a new venture for both commands. In an often-quoted snippet from his papers, Rodman declared:

I realized that the British fleet had had three years of actual warfare and knew the game from the ground floor up; that while we might know it theoretically, there would be a great deal to learn practically. There could not be two independent commands in one force if our work was to be harmonious, and the only logical course was to amalgamate our ships and serve under the command of the British commander-in-chief.

Rodman, leading by example, reported swiftly to commander of the Grand Fleet, Admiral Sir David Beatty, immediately on landing. Although Beatty could be very critical of the American ships' performance, he always kept his criticism quiet and limited to those who needed to know. Both men at the top worked well together and formed a lasting friendship. The impact of this budding relationship filtered down through the ranks, and many long-term friendships were forged.

Rodman's first foray with the British fleet showed that some immediate adjustments needed to be made. One of these was the poor condition of American torpedoes. The American device had a range of about 7,500 yards; "the policy of the commander in chief, Grand Fleet 2, is to open an engagement at maximum range and keep beyond the enemy's torpedo range (15,000 yards)." The difference could be fatal, as the fleets closed in for more accurate firing but were probably beyond the effective range of the American torpedoes. Since the torpedoes were useless under those circumstances, Rodman recommended that they close off the torpedo rooms, bulkhead closed tightly, and use them as flotation chambers. He also reported to Admiral Benson that the guns were too open to the weather and lacked proper protection for the operating crews. He then stated, "Unless adequate weather protection be furnished, whether this be in the form of splinter-proof, blast-proof, or wind and weather-proof shelter is a matter to be considered." Obviously, efficiency fell off rapidly under such adverse conditions. Captain Thomas Washington of the *Florida* made note of the fact that some of the British ships' guns had been made watertight with the addition of "shutters." Water, especially during high seas, often entered the gun batteries through openings (called windows) and fouled the weapon and ammunition. It was a small but significant design problem in the older, coal-burning vessels sent by the United States on request of the British, who lacked oil enough for more modern oil-burning ships.

According to British standard practice, concentration of fire was one of the most important aspects of their battle tactics; however, the American ships *Delaware* and *Florida* were inconsistent and of little help to each other.

Their combined fire was too erratic to be effective in April 1918. *Florida*'s gun shutters flew off, thereby allowing the sea to come in to such an extent that the ship had to drop out of formation to repair the damage or face serious flooding issues. Under war conditions, this would not have been allowed, and its performance would have been a detriment to the fleet. In May, the *Florida* went to Newcastle upon Tyne for docking and fitting for paravanes, an anti-mine device that deflected mines from the front of the vessel. In June, the steering gear failed to work and put the *Florida* in the vicinity of a minefield, but luckily, control was resumed, and the patrol was finished safely. Two things did improve for the *Florida*: its shooting accuracy and dispersal of shots were vastly improved and made Captain Washington a happy man. Admiral Rodman, however, was not pleased with the engine room's spare compartment, as he had been struck twice by a protruding door handle; as Bennett noted, Rodman was a large man.

Aside from the Scandinavian convoys, where the *Florida* and its mates served at least four times, one important duty the Sixth Battle Squadron had was to guard the mine-laying operation for the North Sea Mine Barrage. This was a vast and timely undertaking, and it had to close off the North Sea route to submarines attempting to enter the North Atlantic. The barrage was to stretch from Norway to Scotland, about 250 miles long and 900 feet deep, and it took about 400,000 mines to complete. It was a dangerous occupation for the mine layers, since the new explosive TNT was being used. When

Captain Washington and the officers of the USS *Florida. Author's collection.*

completed, it was one of the greatest undertakings of its kind in history. Commanding one of the flimsy mine layers was the future rear admiral D. Pratt Mannix. Taking command of the *Jefferson*, the young commander set forth to lay part of this vast enterprise; it was a prized idea of Assistant Secretary of the Navy Franklin D. Roosevelt.

It was a dangerous job, not only because of the new and volatile explosive, but also because the area of the world where this barrage was laid was one of the most storm-prone, cold and difficult areas of the sea. Add to these problems the possible presence of German submarines, and the job becomes very dangerous indeed. It was part of the Sixth Battle Squadron's job to form a protective barrier around these mine layers. It was not a continuous duty, since the mines were new, untried and subject to exploding prematurely, sometimes on land. This latter problem forced the designers to hold off laying the mines for weeks, until the problem could be fixed and mine laying resumed. Some naval authorities doubted if these mines could do the job, but according to Mannix's account, they spotted the bodies of several German sailors floating on the rough sea. These mine-laying operations often took five days to a week to complete just one section of the barrage. The guard duty—if it can be called such—was rotated among the British and American battleships. Why use the heavy hitters? This was simply done to discourage the High Seas Fleet from sending out a force of battle cruisers to destroy the mine-laying fleet. The Great North Sea Mine Barrage was never completed, not because of the dangers, but because the armistice was signed before the work was done. It was a valiant and dangerous mission and is part of the legacy of the Sixth Battle Squadron, including the USS *Florida*.

There were many meetings between the British and Americans before the United States entered the war, and many revolved around what to do about the submarine menace. Enough had been hashed over that by April 5, 1917, Arthur Balfour, Secretary Daniels, the imperial war cabinet and the general board of the navy all agreed that the number-one priority for the naval units must be the elimination of the U-boat threat. As David Trask reminds us, "Fears, prejudices, and suspicions had slowly receded in face of the mounting U-boat threat, a circumstance that at least cleared the way for direct negotiations as soon as the United States became a belligerent." The debate in the United States was not just about the U-boat menace but about the type of ships needed to defeat it and the High Seas Fleet should it ever escape into the North Atlantic. Admiral Benson preferred to continue with the capital ship program, one that the general board hoped would help the United States build a navy equal to the combined size of the German and Japanese fleets in typical Mahan fashion. Others, notably Admiral Sims, would prefer the construction of "screening forces," which included numerous destroyers, cruisers and battle cruisers. Time and money were both against the large program, but the construction of smaller vessels, which were designed with antisubmarine warfare in mind, would be more feasible in the immediate future and would assist with the convoys that were assembling at the docks. It would also meet the British need for escorts for the convoys that were agreed on.

Benson, like others of the "old school," was most concerned about the protection of the United States, especially along the coasts. This may not have simply been a military need. Benson and others surely recalled the clamor for defense structures and ships to protect America against the mighty Spanish fleet. As a result, immediately after the United States declared war, Benson assigned roughly 30 percent of the destroyer force and a number of cruisers and armed merchantmen to defend the coast. Sims received the other 70 percent and immediately assigned them to Queenstown, Ireland, under the operational control of the Royal Navy under Admiral Sir Lewis Bayly. Bayly was known for his gruff manner, stern discipline and no-nonsense attitude toward war. He had crossed swords with Lord Fisher and John Jellicoe in his past and survived the battles, and in the case of Jellicoe, he kept his respect. How would Sims deal with someone who had many of his own characteristics? The answer was found in their mutual respect, mutual admiration and lifelong friendship. They worked well as a team, and Sims was able to assign some of the navy's top minds to Queenstown and Gibraltar, the two main bases for the escorts. The escorts were for both the incoming and outgoing convoys and antisubmarine duty when called on. Late in the summer of 1917, the Gibraltar command, under Admiral Albert Niblack, received a number of smaller escort vessels, including six U.S. Coast Guard cutters: the *Ossipee*, *Seneca*, *Yamacraw*, *Algonquin*, *Manning* and *Tampa*. The *Tampa* and the former USCGC *Tallapoosa* had already seized the Austrian ship *Borneo*, the first overt action by the coast guard in the war.

The Queenstown command from the American side was given to Commander Joseph Taussig, who brought the first six destroyers to Irish port, the first contribution made to the Allied cause in the war. Queenstown was a very strategic position, as it guarded the "western approaches" to England. In the words of Elting Morison, "Through these approaches passed almost all of the traffic coming from the Americas with the elements of war upon which England's survival depended." At Queenstown, there had been a great deal of friction between London (Jellicoe and friends) and Bayly, mostly over small things and differences in personnel, or lack thereof, for the base. Bayly had not had a holiday in over two years and had not been promoted to the position of commander in chief at Queensland, as others with less service and experience had been. Sims, through his friendship with Jellicoe and with the power of persuasion of the first lord of the admiralty Sir Edward Carson, was able to get both done on Bayly's behalf. According to Morison, this greatly improved the relations between London and Queenstown and helped cement the new friendship between Bayly and Sims. Another appointment by Sims, the chief of staff in Ireland, was Captain Joel R. Poinsett Pringle. It was a marvelous choice, as Pringle had the tact, knowledge and polish to handle almost any situation. He was efficient, orderly and punctual, and he so impressed the critical Bayly that he referred to Pringle as the "beau ideal" of a naval officer.

Thirty-six submarine chasers were added to the fleet in Queenstown, but they were only suitable for assignments close to shore, as they were not the most seaworthy of vessels. Bayly was skeptical but loved having them around because they "have lots of pluck." One final note concerning the famed relationship between Bayly and Sims concerns the lady of the house in the Bayly residence, Miss Violet Voysey, the admiral's beloved niece. She took a sincere liking to Sims and many of his officers and was often considered "in league" with Sims for the benefit of "Uncle Lewis."

There were other bottlenecks that hampered the operations delivering food and troops into war-torn Europe, especially France. The harbors on the western coast of France south of the English Channel offered an almost direct line to the interior of France. Brest, Lorient, Saint-Nazaire and the Gironde Estuary offered the best options for development, but none had been developed to handle the amount of goods and troops that arrived when the United States moved into full gear. Along the Bay of Biscay, near Brest, the tides were dangerous but manageable, but the submarines were another story. The western ports had to be protected if the U.S. forces and supplies were to arrive at the front lines. Two types of convoys operated out of Brest, the transatlantic traffic, which involved larger, more demanding vessels as far as space and depth were concerned, and the shallower, lighter draft vessels to convoy the coastal port-to-port movements. To answer the immediate needs, the U.S. Navy sent a handful of converted private vessels (yachts) to Brest in early June. The USS *Noma* was the flagship of the small flotilla of six vessels, and it was commanded by Captain William B. Fletcher, who was detached in October and replaced by Rear Admiral Henry B. Wilson. The USS *Noma* had the honor of being the first vessel to encounter a German

German U-Boat UB-65. *Image from* History's Greatest War: A Pictorial Narrative, *1919*.

submarine. Later, under Wilson's command, the number of ships on the various convoy duties was increased to a total of thirty-five destroyers, five torpedo boats, eighteen yachts, nine minesweepers, eight tugs and other assorted vessels. This command had the proud record of never losing one transport vessel or life during its tenure. Some ships were sunk and lost to the service; however, none were troop transports or armed naval vessels. Admiral Wilson constantly complained of not having enough vessels to do the job, but he apparently successfully proceeded to do so anyway. He was a constant thorn in Sims's side, but he was not replaced and was acknowledged for his command's success.

The other major convoy base was the British island of Gibraltar, the crossroads of the Mediterranean and the primary bottleneck that had to be controlled and not dominated by the German submarine campaign. It was the key passageway for all colonial traffic in either troops, food or other materials. If it was so vital to the success of the empire, why didn't the Grand Fleet station at least some of its prized battleships there and use its destroyers to control the submarine threat? Historian I.T. Greig has summed up three major reasons for this strange behavior. First, there was the theoretical obsession with the decisive battle concept called the Trafalgar Effect. The main fleet's reason for existence was to seek out the enemy and destroy its fleet before it could cause harm to the home country. This was the predominant thought of the admiralty prior to and throughout most of the war. Second, the Grand Fleet had been so dominant throughout its recent history that it had little to fear from a "weaker" naval force, like that of Germany. It forced the opponent into a *guerre de course*–style of commerce raiding, which was easily defeated in earlier conflicts. Third, there was little recognition by the admiralty that submarines could be a threat to Britain's commerce as they had been during the war. So heavy were the losses of commercial vessels and other ships that by October 1916, Sir John Jellicoe came to the realization that it was no longer a victory over the High Seas Fleet that mattered most but the defeat of the submarine force. Even with these facts staring the admiralty in the face, they refused to think a convoy system was practical.

In December 1916, the admiralty created an antisubmarine division of the staff, with Rear Admiral A.L. Duff as its director. The losses continued to mount until April 1917, when nearly nine hundred thousand tons of shipping were lost. That was the situation for Jellicoe and the admiralty when Sims made his entrance into the debate. How serious were the losses? As Professor A.J. Marder stated, "The chance of an ocean-going steamer leaving the United Kingdom and returning safely was but one in four." Britain was losing what German admiral Karl Doenitz called "the tonnage war," and they were losing it big time.

The American command at Gibraltar, starting in April 1918, was in the capable hands of Rear Admiral Albert P. Niblack, a former roommate of Sims at the naval academy. The two had remained friends throughout the years, and their correspondence during the war was commonly "Dear Billy to Dear Nibs." Admiral Niblack had a great deal of experience prior to this appointment. He had been in the service for nearly forty-seven years when he was placed on the retirement list in 1923. At the beginning of his career, he served as a student at the Smithsonian Institute; he was under instruction for exploring prior to his transfer to Alaska, where he was involved in surveying the coastline and exploring the inland of the wilderness. From 1896 until the outbreak of the Spanish-American War, he served as the naval attaché in Berlin, Vienna and Rome. During the war with Spain, he served on the USS *Topeka* as part of the blockading squadron and then transferred to the *Olympia*, where he served in the Philippine Insurrection, including commanding a landing force in the capture of Llo-Llo Straits. He was detached and served on the USS *Castine* in the North China Expeditionary Force during the Boxer Rebellion. He continued serving as an attaché in Berlin and later Buenos Aires, and from 1913 to 1916, he served as the commanding officer of the USS *Michigan*, where he commanded the third seaman's regiment in the occupation of Vera Cruz, Mexico, in 1914. When the war broke out in

1917, he was quickly assigned to command the Second Squadron, Patrol Force, Atlantic Fleet, with the USS *Birmingham* as his flagship. The station base was Gibraltar. It was to be a sensitive assignment and one of the most important in the war. Niblack had to tackle the submarine problem, keep the Strait of Gibraltar open and oversee convoys going north to Great Britain and across the Mediterranean. It was a demanding job.

One of the earliest memorandums sent to Niblack from the "force commander" (Sims) made sure everyone in the command knew their main assignments:

> *You should impress on all commanding officers* [the] *necessity for taking the offensive against submarines whenever they are sighted or their location is known. Force instructions on this subject are in course of preparation, as several instances have arisen both in our own service and in allied services, in which an escorting vessel has abandoned the attack on an enemy submarine for reasons that it thought its convoy was in no further immediate danger from that particular enemy.*

Whatever it took to ensure the escape of the convoy was justified, especially attacking the invading submarine. Sims was known for not micromanaging his forces, and he left leeway for his commanders to exercise on-the-spot judgements. He expected action to be taken and encouraged his commanders to drive off and sink the opposition.

Like Wilson at Brest, Niblack also had problems getting enough trained men, especially officers, sent to his command. Sims knew the frustration of having to do a seemingly impossible job with few tools in the box. On April 12, 1918, he wrote "Nibs" that he was having his assistant write an explanation of why the navy department ordered some of his officers to Queenstown and other northern bases without sending him any replacements. As a way of consolation, Sims noted, "Since the very beginning, the yachts on the French coast have been operating with only one commissioned officer on board. As you may imagine, I have protested very energetically against this and have told the department that if that condition of affairs resulted in disaster some of these days, there would be no possible defense." He further reminded his colleague that the promise of more destroyers that had been sent out in January had "fallen down nearly completely." Sims also noted that he had been promised ten destroyers per month beginning in January. "You know what has happened." Basically, the navy had not provided or received from its contractors the said destroyers, nor had any of the 110-foot chasers

The Bevins brothers aboard the coast guard cutter USS *Tampa. Courtesy of the State Archives of Florida, Bevins Papers.*

arrived. But there were signs of hope; forty-eight of the chasers were, at that time, in Bermuda and on their way to the Azores. In the meantime, coast guard cutters, converted yachts and other assorted craft had to suffice. Some of these proved to be of value in patrolling the Spanish coast, where the fishermen were suspected of supplying German submarines and smuggling supplies to the mainland.

From New York, Algy Bevins wrote to his mother from the USS *Tampa*, saying that she need not worry: "You folks need not worry, as we are going with a fleet of first-class vessels and have some French sub-chasers." He then reminded his mother, "We are not in any more danger than you are and not as much as you were the last time I saw you." Algy and his brother Arthur were aboard the *Tampa* doing "their bit" for the country and making $38.40 per month each; both were sending $30.00 home every payday. The main function of the cutters was to escort convoys between Gibraltar and the British Isles. The *Tampa* was originally christened *Miami* but had spent so much of its time in Tampa that the city kind of adopted it. When the U.S. Revenue Service and the U.S. Lifesaving Service combined to create the new U.S. Coast Guard in January 1915, it was the third service under the mandate of the U.S. Treasury Department. It also changed the official name of the *Miami* to *Tampa* on February 1, 1916. When the war broke out, the coast guard was assigned to the navy, where it remained until after the armistice. These sturdy cutters were almost ideal for the service they were assigned to render. Built to withstand rough seas and move quickly, the cutter was well designed and carried a crew of over one hundred men, not including officers. According to Algy Bevins, they had something else: "a fine cat on board for a mascot." Bevins said, "All the world like Munce, only we call him 'Red.'"

The *Tampa* was built in 1912 at Newport News, Virginia, for $250,000 (about $6.5 million in 2019) and was launched on February 10, 1912. It was 190 feet long, with a 32-foot beam and a 14-foot draft below the water. It was equipped with a 1,300-horsepower engine that easily made 20 knots and more when needed. It was armed with three six-pounder rapid-fire guns, two 76-mm naval guns, two machine guns and four 3.50-caliber guns. It was also equipped to throw depth charges and roll them from the deck. It was well armed and commanded by veteran Captain Charles Satterlee. At the time of the *Tampa*'s appointment to Gibraltar, Captain Satterlee was forty-three years old and a veteran with over twenty years of experience. The captain was a graduate of the Revenue Cutter Service (RCS) School in New Bedford, Massachusetts; he graduated and was commissioned as a

U.S. Coast Guard cutter USS *Tampa*. *Courtesy of the State Archives of Florida.*

third lieutenant on January 17, 1898. During the Spanish-American War of 1898, the revenue cutters were assigned to assist the navy in the blockade of Cuba, and Third Lieutenant Satterlee was assigned to duty on the RCS cutter *Levi Woodbury*. This vessel served as part of the blockade of Havana Harbor in cooperation with Admiral Sampson's North Atlantic Squadron. Satterlee joined the crew of the *Miami* at Key West on December 9, 1915. One look at the pictures of this beautiful ship gives one the impression of speed and a daring nature.

The *Tampa* had an enviable record escorting convoys out of Gibraltar. According the records cited by Admiral Sims, dated October 2, 1918, the *Tampa* averaged 3,566 miles per month and was underway 50.4 percent of the time it was on station. It escorted eighteen convoys between Gibraltar and the United Kingdom and was never disabled. It was an efficient vessel that was well captained and had an excellent ship's spirit. Unfortunately, it made one mistake—if such it was. On the evening of September 26, 1918, it was escorting a convoy, Convoy HG-107, consisting of thirty-two ships, to the United Kingdom. When approaching the Irish Sea and England's Bristol Channel, the *Tampa* left the convoy and headed toward Milford Haven to drop off sixteen British dock workers and military personnel and to possibly refuel. According to the log of Captain Wolf-Hans Hertwig, the submarine UB-91 spotted the cutter around 7:40 p.m. and launched its one stern torpedo at 8:15 p.m. It was the perfect shot and hit portside amidships. About two minutes later, after the initial explosion, a second explosion took place. Captain Hertwig speculated that the second explosion came from the ignition of the depth charges in the hold. The beautiful *Tampa* went down in two minutes. There were no survivors; 131 people lost their lives in the tragedy. It was the "greatest single loss in combat fatal casualties for the United States Navy and Coast Guard during World War I." There were three sets of brothers aboard the *Tampa* when it met its fate, and 24 members of the crew were from the ship's namesake city; 35 of the crewmembers were from the state of Florida. It was a sad day for the Sunshine State and the nation as a whole.

One final question was answered after the war with the log of UB-91. Yes, the submarine surfaced and looked for survivors and found none. The command at Gibraltar sent out two vessels to look for survivors on September 27 and 28 but to no avail. Only two bodies were ever recovered, but neither were identified. Very little debris was found near the wreckage site, except for a partial mast with a life jacket attached and a couple of packing crates with the name of the ship. It was a sad day, and this is reflected in the memorandum sent by Admiral Niblack to his friend Admiral Sims:

> *The loss of the Tampa is the worst thing that has come to us yet, as she had just gone north from a complete refit and been commended for having had an uneventful career with every kind of commendation for efficiency. I was holding Captain Scally* [a Baltimore native], *the Executive Officer, in reserve for a good command, but he was particularly anxious to remain on the Tampa, where he was very happy.*

7

AND THE BOYS WROTE HOME

Lives and Letters of Greater Tampa Bay Soldiers in World War I

I n John Harllee's book *The Marine from Manatee: A Tradition of Rifle Marksmanship*, he tells the following story of his ancestor Major William Curry Harllee. The "Maje" Harllee and naval captain Charles P. Plunkett were on their way to the navy department and were passing the White House on the day the United States declared war. They noticed a guard outside of the doors carrying a rifle when Harllee stated, "The trouble is, Captain, that those American soldiers who are supposed to be guarding the President probably couldn't hit the broad side of a barn with those rifles they're carrying" The captain was surprised and commented, "Maje, you're crazy!" The major then challenged the captain to ask the young soldier how good he was with the gun.

"Son," said the captain, "How good are you with that rifle you're carrying?"

The sentry responded, "Don't know, sir. Never shot one yet."

"What?" Captain Plunkett exclaimed with startled disbelief. Then, "Is that rifle loaded?"

"Yes, sir," said the sentry. "The corporal, he loads 'em for us every morning when we go on duty. But he locks 'em, and he orders us not to fool with the lock."

The captain then took the gun from the soldier, examined it and returned it, noting its loaded state. "Now," said Major Harllee, "you see what I mean when I fight for rifle ranges. Now you see what's guarding the president of the United States in wartime. A soldier with a gun he's got orders not to shoot! And he doesn't know how to shoot it. No man has any business with a rifle unless he can shoot straight!" The captain, who was in charge of the office of gunnery exercises and engineering performances in the navy department, then gave Major Harllee orders to build the rifle ranges that were needed. Harllee did just that, and by the end of the war, at least twenty-five were in operation. Whether it's true or not, the story makes the point; the stories of shooting expertise by Americans of that day were mythological.

Noted World War I historian Edward Coffman gives a similar example, noting the arrival of the first American troops in Paris on July 4, 1917. The commanding officer of the unit, Sidney C. Graves, remembered, "The officers were afraid of the showing we might make since we had so many recruits....These men couldn't even slope arms. They were even more dangerous with a loaded rifle." The examples of men who could not shoot are so numerous that it would be too repetitive to give all them here. The only problem the American forces did not have was that Pershing truly believed his troops could outshoot the effete European armies and defeat them in open warfare. But there was only one William Curry Harllee and not nearly enough rifle ranges, thus was the unprepared nature of American forces when President Woodrow Wilson called the nation to arms.

Wilson called for a tremendous increase in men under arms in April 1917, and the nation responded with increased enlistments, a growing national guard and more than two million draftees, the first such draft since the Civil War. The problem then was not the number of men but how to arm them, train them and ship them to the battlefronts of Europe. At the beginning of the war, much of the weapons production was slated for European allies, not the U.S. Army and Marines. The highest production rate of small arms that could be obtained by 1918 was about one thousand rifles per day. There was no production of machine guns capable of even training the few squads allowed per division. Many machine gunners did not see a real machine gun or fire one until they reached France. The same could be said for the Stokes mortar platoons; many never fired one until they were on the front lines. James Rainey quoted in *The Official History of the 28th Division*, "Rifles, automatic rifles, trench mortars, .37-, .57- and .155-mm guns used in combat were not secured until the division reached France. We had only one bayonet for every third man, which meant changing for drill....The division had but a few gas masks, which made training slow and difficult." In the matter of artillery, it should be noted that the U.S. Army had not decided, as of July 1917, just what type or size of guns should be manufactured for the army's use. When the army started showing up in France, it had to borrow the 75-mm guns and the 155-mm guns from the French. It also did

Machine gun practice. *Author's collection.*

not have any tanks, airplanes or sufficient machine guns for each regiment, and a majority of the men and equipment they did have had been shipped in British bottoms. To say the United States was not prepared for a major conflict would be an understatement.

With few of the vital instruments of death available to train its army, the U.S. military's leadership emphasized physical fitness, drill and use of the bayonet to occupy its men. The poor condition of many recruits and draftees made the requirement of physical fitness a priority for the trainers. As Coffman had noted, even in the brief Mexican expedition led by Pershing, of the National Guard units that were called out, few were up to strength in numbers or physical condition. Most had difficulties finding recruits to replace those who failed to pass the physicals or show up for duty. "Regular army observers," it was noted, "considered the state of training of nearly all of the units entering active service as little more than rudimentary." The draftees and volunteers were sent to training camps that had been established throughout the country.

The smallness of the regular army prior to the declaration of war made finding suitable trainers for the new force a nearly impossible task. Since many of the noncommissioned officers had been promoted to lieutenant and captain positions, the strain of finding suitable replacements for training purposes fell on the individual units and the remaining NCOs. The lack of tactical doctrine limited the type of training these new "officers" could

Our boys in camp. *Author's collection.*

offer to the men. The emphasis in these camps was on physical conditioning (like the dreaded twelve-mile hike), group drills following the manual, learning the rudimentary elements of military customs and life and personal healthcare. Visits to nearby towns were limited, and houses of questionable character were put out of business. Liquor sales were forbidden in and around the camps. Classwork was one of the main requirements, primarily drawings and examples of real weapons, their breakdowns, cleaning rules and maintenance. Not to be forgotten was the work with entrenching tools, especially the faithful shovel. Many soldiers cursed this vicious object; however, they soon found the simple tool to be their best friend on the front lines when the bullets whizzed by or the warbirds passed overhead.

The camps the men were sent to were seldom completed by the time the first arrivals disembarked. Camp Wadsworth, just outside of Spartanburg, South Carolina, was in a very primitive state when part of the Seventh Infantry showed up. In addition to doing the daily calisthenics, the troops took turns at constructing a road into the camp and became experts in handling shovels and picks. Grubbing stumps in the Carolina sun and practicing digging trenches until dark put the men in relatively good condition. After digging the trenches, the units took seventy-two-hour rotations manning the newly constructed system, similar to what they would experience in France. Camp Greene, located just outside of Charlotte, North Carolina, was accessible to rail and road transportation. In the first wave of trainees, the majority of the corps were from Massachusetts and some were from South Carolina. As the war progressed, troops from all over the country, including Florida, sent men to the camp for training. There were also facilities for the Black troops to train since, like almost all of the camps, segregation was the rule. With the aid of the soldiers, especially the engineers, the camp was constructed in ninety days and included stables, a bakery, laundry, hospital, chapel, post office and facilities for the YMCA, Knights of Columbus and the Red Cross. Camp Sheridan, where the Alabama National Guard mobilized, was located just outside of Montgomery. There, the men underwent physicals, and anywhere between 25 and 30 percent were rejected for insufficient weight (common among poor Whites and Blacks), venereal diseases, bad teeth, tuberculosis and heart disease. Since many were from the poor, rural areas of Alabama (and neighboring states) many had never seen a doctor or dentist in their lives. The training routine there was similar to other facilities and included, for the first three weeks, physical drills, "school of the soldier" (lessons on what was expected of each and every man in uniform, including saluting lieutenants, saying "yes, sir," and "no, sir," et cetera) and the footwork for bayonet drills. Instruction also included the nomenclature of guns, care of guns and assembling a pack. Some time was also spent on hygiene and sexually transmitted diseases, army rations, pay schedules, et cetera. By the end of week three, regular guard duty was part of the new routine.

Camp Wadsworth in Spartanburg, South Carolina. *Author's collection.*

Camp Wheeler was the main destination for most of the Florida troops, especially the national guard, which was formerly known as the Second Florida Infantry and commanded by Colonel Albert H. Blanding. These men came from cities all over the state, including Gainesville, Orlando, Palatka, Lakeland, Plant City, Arcadia, Wauchula and Tampa. They were joined there by contingents from Miami, Key West and West Palm Beach. Tampa sent its men off to the strains of "Yankee Doodle" and feasted on 344 box lunches provided by the local Red Cross and consumed in the DeSoto Hotel's breakfast room. The sendoff included other organizations standing at attention, such as the Boy Scouts, the coastal artillery companies, the Hillsborough County Guard and the junior naval reserve. With full bellies, stout hearts and dreams of glory, the Florida boys headed to Camp Wheeler, where it was estimated they would be trained at a cost of nearly $3 million.

Writing for the *St. Andrews Bay News*, Phil B. West answered many questions regarding the training and living conditions for the Florida boys. His experience with the Fifty-Sixth Depot Brigade (formerly part of Company M, First Florida Infantry) provided much of his background. Writing under the column heading "With Our Men at Camp Wheeler," West explained that the depot brigade was, in reality, a training facility for both men and animals, not just a military depot where the tools of war were stored and shipped. The war department had directed that draftees from Florida, Alabama and Georgia would be ordered to Camp Wheeler for training and "veterans" of the national guard would do much of the instruction. The units that were already there were included in the newly created Thirty-First Division, commanded by General Hayden. Colonel Blanding remained in command of the Fifty-Sixth Depot Brigade.

On the deep, rich red clay of the rolling hills of central Georgia, Camp Wheeler was described as being in the high rolling hills with plenty of pine and hardwood available for construction. It was also very dusty in the hot, dry summer sun. It was totally different when it rained and became almost impassable because of the sticky nature of the clay. The camp's water supply, along with the electricity that was needed in the hospitals, was provided by the city of Macon. The site was located on a high eminence to take advantage of the healthful winds. The land was producing cotton when the first troops arrived, and much of it was in full boll. Some of this crop had to be sacrificed to make room for the soldiers. To avoid some of the obvious errors of the Spanish-American War camps, the kitchen areas were at the opposite end of the camp from the showers and latrines. Inoculations for typhoid and typhus fevers, spinal meningitis and other diseases were required, and the troops, as noted before, were often lectured on health matters and personal cleanliness. West also noted that the food was pretty good and said, "The men who kick about their chow were, in 99 cases out of 100, unused to such good fare at home." Unlike what they were to experience in France, the men were provided with iron cots with springs, two woolen blankets and bedding sacks filled with clean hay at frequent intervals. He also noted that the YMCA had five buildings at the camp, and they provided free stationery for writing home, and stamps were sold to the men to cover the postage. Chaplains were present every Sunday and many other days to meet the men's spiritual needs and keep up the morale, especially among those who became homesick, as it was the first time many had ever left their hometowns. Interestingly, pillows were not provided, and West made a pitch for families or friends to send a "warm, single-size comfort, preferably a dark colored one" for the cooler nights ahead. Little did West know that the winter of 1917–18 would be the coldest on record at that point. Hopefully, his advice was followed.

Not all was pleasing and progressing at Camp Wheeler. Like all large gatherings of men and women, contagious diseases visited the camp. On November 5, 1917, the *Florida Times-Union* reported the deaths of four men from pneumonia in one day at Camp Wheeler. Sergeant St. John noted the outbreak of measles prior to a review of the troops by the governor of Georgia. The fall of 1917 saw the first outbreak of influenza that would, over the course of a year, mutate into the deadliest pandemic in world history. The camps, and later the front-line trenches, were perfect breeding grounds for such diseases, and a watchful eye had to be constantly kept up to prevent each outbreak from turning into something much worse. The crippling effects of these outbreaks are noteworthy, not just in the recorded deaths, but in the changes required by commanders in meeting their military goals. Attacks had to be delayed, troops were moved rapidly from one front to another, the timing of attacks were changed to meet the new conditions, the transfers of

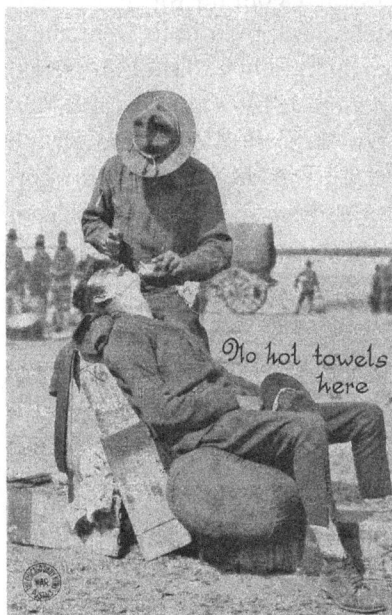

"No Hot Towels Here." *Author's collection.*

supplies from one area to another had to be rearranged and logistics became a nightmare to those seeking to move men, troops and animals from one area to another. The spread of disease changed the course of battles and subjected nearby civilian populations to their ravages.

The cold weather of the winter of 1917–18 made it desirable for the troops to get warmer clothing and other comforts either from home or the Red Cross. At Camp Wheeler, the Red Cross provided sweaters to the troops, which were gratefully received and used. These may have been worn by the men as they sat down to a rather plentiful Christmas dinner. While enjoying the repast, Captain Vestal gave a record of Company E from the time it was organized as a unit in the coastal artillery to its service on the Mexican border, chasing Pancho Villa and his band. Of the unit that served on this frontier, only 44 of 183 men were then in service. Then colonel and later brigadier general Blanding was the commanding officer. This history was a means of building up the esprit de corps of the unit, something all armies attempt. Belonging to a unit that had such an illustrious service record gave men pride in their company.

Tampa's contingent at Camp Wheeler also wrote home to the local newspaper in the column "With the Tampa Boys at Camp Wheeler, Ga." Written by Sergeants Epping and Will Davis, their column was newsy and meant to entertain as well as inform. They noted that their units were living in tents with wooden floors, not wooden barracks. They told of the usual cakes, cookies, et cetera that were sent to the men by their families and how much was (or wasn't) shared. Some of the letters received by the boys were not the pleasant kind that were usually noted, as in the case of Corporal Wheeler, who had "just received a letter from some fair damsel and from the actions which he is going through, he must have received the 'grand bounce.'" (These were later known as "Dear John" letters.) The usual hijinks were also reported, and they made it known that it was not safe for one of them to go to bed ahead of the others. "It pays to keep your eyes open," they warned, "while in the aforesaid tent [we know]." The humor found in the column is best illustrated by the story of one of them who tried his first mango, which created a small sensation. They reported that the gentlemen said it would be his last mango "until he gets a bathing suit." Life at Camp Wheeler was hard work and training, but it appears to never have been too dull for the boys from Tampa.

Like other southern military camps, Camp Wheeler was a segregated affair with separate facilities for Black and White troops. Its situation in a former cotton plantation must have had an impact on the "colored"

Zack Crumpton (*far right, second row*). *Used with the permission of Mr. Zack Waters of Rome, Georgia, from his private collection.*

troops, as they were called. One of the only real benefits these men received was the mail from home, since most never had such a luxury as free rural delivery to their homes. If they were at home, the mail was often delivered to the plantation owners, who read them their own mail since most had little if any education. This created some problems for the recipients, as the owners, if the men received their draft notice during picking season, often withheld the information until the sheriff or other officer of the law came to enforce the draft notice or put the men in jail. Sometimes, the landowner would withhold the information until after the harvest was in then inform the sheriff himself to collect the fifty-dollar reward for turning in a "draft dodgers." Draft exemptions for field workers were freely given to plantation owners, and they often applied for them in the workers' names without informing the individuals. It must be remembered that almost all of the draft boards were controlled by the local White elite. The South had the highest rate of draft dodging in the nation, which is not surprising given the circumstances described.

Florida did get some training camps established within its boundaries, but they were mostly specialist training facilities, like the naval air station, the pilot's training school in Dade County and Carlstrom and Dorr in Arcadia. The largest training facility in Florida was Camp Joseph E. Johnston near Jacksonville. It took a mammoth lobbying effort by the City of Jacksonville and Senator Duncan U. Fletcher to procure this quartermaster's base. The first contingent of 1,600 men arrived at the post at the end of November 1917. The camp was expected to reach a maximum of fifteen to twenty-five thousand troops by early 1918. As the main focus was the quartermaster corps, the training, in addition to the physical aspects, included all facets of supply and loading. Classwork included concepts of shipping long distances, where and how to procure difficult items and working within railroad schedules. One of the more unique training groups were the truck drivers. As the *Florida Times-Union* noted on October 16, 1917, the men were to be trained as "experts in handling this equipment" and moving men and supplies over long distances.

Captain J.W. O'Mahoney had been in the service as a member of the New York National Guard. At one time, he commanded a twelve-inch battery for the coastal artillery unit. He was also, the newspaper noted, "Engaged in automobile engineering as a private occupation and studied the motor transportation as applied to army use. Even before the famous tanks came into use, he designed and built several desirable tractors for army work." For the purposes of the army, O'Mahoney sought to train his men in all facets of transportation and equipment. The idea behind this training was to move men and machines "across rough country under all conditions of weather and terrain." The equipment trains were made up of thirty-three trucks, averaging a mile and a half in length. They were, in this training, to take these trains between the camp and Black Point, a distance of about fifty miles. The men would then learn the details of handling the equipment and know how to build bridges and roads from the materials at hand. Nothing was allowed to slow down the delivery of men, machines and supplies. The only complaint from the men would have been lack of timely pay:

[Sung to the tune of "I've Been Working on the Railroad."]
It' all we do is sign the payroll
All we do is sign the payroll
All we do is sign the payroll,
But we don't get one d----d cent.

Like all camps, Camp Johnston had its rain, mosquitoes and high temperatures to accompany the lack of mosquito netting, bedding and other discomforts.

The trip "across the pond" was one of the most unique experiences for many of the men, some of whom had never seen the Atlantic Ocean.

Top: Wagon Company 302, Lieutenant F.J. Rogers, Company Commander. in Camp Johnston, Florida. *Author's collection.*

Bottom: Singing Sammies. *Author's collection.*

Furgerson Jones, in writing for the *Punta Gorda Herald*, noted, "We had a nice trip across the pond, though two submarines caused some excitement. Both were sunk by the convoying destroyers." The passage of Clair Jones and Will Austin was not so smooth. Will's diary noted that nearly everyone on the *Huron* got seasick, which made for an uncomfortable first leg of the voyage. They took a southern route to avoid the German submarines that were supposedly in the area. Will also noted that there was no smoking at night; the boredom was heavy and long and the tempers were short during the trip. When they reached the Bay of Biscay, things got worse: "A terrible storm struck the Bay of Biscay, or 'Sailor's Grave,' as it is better known. I was on guard that night, got a drenching and damaged my arm. Ruined my rifle." The diarist observed more damage: "One sailor went overboard from destroyer 38 and was lost. One went overboard from our escort, the cruiser *Montana*, but was picked up after being in the water 20 minutes. One gun crew (four men) from our ship was lost and six men of the Sixth Engineers. Twelve lifeboats were smashed to bits and we went without food for 36 hours." When the *Huron* docked at St. Marzan on December 23, many of the men were still sick from the voyage and remained on board through Christmas. One of the more interesting observations about the crossing was the landing at Brest, France, of over 125,000 men "of all nationalities, including Chinese and negroes from South Africa." It should be noted that the convoy system was highly effective in preventing attacks on the troop transports, and none of these ships and their valuable cargo were lost during the American involvement.

On landing, most of the troops were sent off to further training under the watchful eyes of either French or British instructors. Most of these instructors were front-line veterans and were there to give their sage advice based on their experiences. The men were shipped to their training stations in forty-and-eights. In the winter of 1917–18, this was not a comfortable mode of travel, especially since the American forces had not been issued proper clothing for the weather. Will Austin bluntly observed:

> We only had our light shoes. Our gloves lasted just three days. And none of us had any caps. Many had the ears frozen. Not having proper shoes, our feet got soaked through; and as the fires were insufficient to get our boots properly dried by night, we found it better not to take our shoes off, but to simply loosen the laces and sleep with them on. Our feet remained warmer, and our shoes dried out a little. Otherwise, the leather was so wet and frozen it was difficult to get them back on.

Before getting the instruction they needed, the group had other duties to attend to, such as building the encampment.

As noted earlier, the training received by the American forces was rudimentary. Most of the training time was spent on exercise and drill, with little practice with the weapons they were to use to attack the enemy. When they got to France, things had to be different. With few machine guns at home, the men were introduced to the guns they were to use throughout the war, in particular, the French Chauchat (often referred to as the "chat-chat") and the Hotchkiss guns. Bayonet drills were also common but not emphasized as they were in the states. Installing the barbed wire defenses and throwing grenades were also stressed as integral parts of the French system of trench warfare.

The French wanted to make the training as realistic as possible, according to Edward Coffman, so the Americans learned to construct trenches, dugouts, bombproofs, et cetera in the French manner. They also taught the soldiers and officers some of the tactics of trench warfare that had worked for them. The instruction went on for eight hours a day, five days a week and half days on Saturdays. There were stretches when the men spent as many as forty-eight hours straight in the trenches, just to give them a taste of what was to come. The instructors quickly got the full attention of the soldiers when they brought out the flamethrowers and taught them how to defend themselves during a gas attack. These physical demonstrations of the power of these latter weapons made a heavy impact on the American doughboy. The French observers of the exercises the men went through noted some glaring faults with the Americans' performance. The failure to pay attention to supply and liaison efforts were pointed out as well as the spacing between men in simulated attack. The closeness of the men in formation would lead to heavy and needless casualties. There was a notable lack of coordination between the artillery and the infantry primarily because joint arms training had not been emphasized in the earlier training. The learning went through all levels of command in addition to that required of the regular troops. Some of the older officers did not pass inspection when it came to the exercises and were either relieved of their commands or sent home to "train" others. One point Pershing made early on in the campaign was that he did not hesitate to remove commanders who did not measure up to his high standards.

The boys from Florida took part in almost every major campaign of the war. They still had their wits and rifles, even if they were borrowed from the French or British, and they had their bayonets. Silly as it seems today, the bayonet was an important part of the psychology of this war, and training in its use continued throughout the Second World War and the Vietnam War. Part of the reason for the use of this weapon was that most of the troops fighting the war were mass armies, similar in content to those of Napoleon. The bayonet filled the gap during frontal assaults that happened to reach the enemy trenches. In the words of historian Rob Engen, "The bayonet itself was thought to give psychological advantages to the infantry soldier in the environment of the trenches on the Western Front that made its use far more practical than the weapon's material effects would otherwise suggest. The bayonet 'made the soldier into a tiger'—and perhaps just as importantly, made the enemy fear him that much more." The fighting in the Second Battle of the Marne, Château-Thierry and at Cantigny seasoned some of the American forces, but the Saint Mihiel and the Meuse-Argonne would test the mettle of all involved.

The fighting at Soissons was described by Sergeant Leonard Eddings in his letters reprinted in the *Tampa Morning Tribune*. In letters to his father that he wrote on returning stateside, Eddings related how his unit was in the trenches for three straight months and was supposed to be in the rear for a rest, which lasted all of three days before new orders sent them marching forward again.

> *We arrived at Soissons July 18 at 4:15 o'clock. At 4:35, we went over the top with the French and British troops on both sides of us for about thirty-five miles. We had over 400 big British tanks and about 600 small French ones. We drove the Germans back nine miles by 11:30 and dug ourselves in to rest. We lost just about forty-five men out of our company of 242. At 4:30 PM, we went over again and succeeded in driving them back for three miles with heavy losses. We had captured about 18,000 prisoners though and killed twice as many. I carried eighty-six prisoners our company captured in the last trench we captured. There were two other men with me. We had to carry them back the twelve miles. It certainly was some awful looking place, men with their heads blown off and bodies cut in half, but to every American lying, there were five Germans. I made the prisoners carry the wounded back; there were American boys who had lain there for four or five hours, wounded severely. Our hospital was doing all it could do. The prisoners seemed glad to work because they could not understand why we hadn't killed them. Lots of places, there was no quarter given.... The next morning, we went over the top again and advanced about a mile, but some of the German tanks drove our tanks back, and as we could not fight tanks with a rifle and bayonet, we had retired about half a mile and dug ourselves in there.*

After two more days of going over the top and gaining ground at high costs, the unit got caught in the crossfire.

The next morning, we carried on. We captured about three miles or more, and here was where the worst fight was. They had sent over 300 machine guns along here, and we had to advance under this in daylight and plain view of the Germans. They mowed us down, and when we reached some of their machine guns, they stuck up their hands and yelled, "Komrad." Of course, you can guess what happened to those Germans. We captured a chateau and got 300 prisoners out of it; one lieutenant colonel and a bunch of junior officers. Here, I killed a lieutenant who would not surrender. I have his pistol. It is a fine one....I was in command of our company when we were relieved and a second lieutenant in command of the battalion. Every company is in charge of a sergeant.

Eddings's thrilling account also brings out the point that the casualty rate among American junior officers, captains and lieutenants was very high. As Professor Schwartz of Western Illinois University recently wrote, "Junior officers and their enlisted soldiers suffered tremendous casualties. One captain, leading an attack against German machine gunners, took his objective but lost all of his junior officers in the process. This was not uncommon, for junior officers in infantry companies suffered casualty rates from 33 to 100 percent." The war department, according to Schwartz's research, "expected a 'wastage' of two thousand officers a month when combat began in earnest." Eddings's account certainly backs up this research.

Dr. Albert Franklin Sarver, serving with the 355th Regiment of the 82nd Division, was also an observer of the Soissons battle. He heard his first shells land around 2:00 p.m. on August 8, when the Germans retaliated for earlier American shelling. On August 9, the Germans sent over a gas barrage in return for an earlier gas shelling by the 82nd Engineers, who had made them a present of eighteen tons of gas bombs. Three hundred men had to be evacuated from the battalion and seven hundred from the division. Sixty men died in this gas attack, which only strengthened the resolve of the Americans to get even with the "Boche." On August 10, the doctor reported, "Gas still remains in the Bois de Jury and low areas. P.C. Conde and low dugouts must be evacuated. Lieutenant Beck and 8 corps men are gassed and evacuated. Captain Durnell comes to Beaumont and I take an advanced position on the Metz road. Accommodates 8 men and 14 rats." Other observations by the physician included the daily dose of 77-mm and "Austrian 88" shellings and the occasional bombing by the German airmen. On August 30, he recorded, "Airplane flights are a daily occurrence, frequently see an observation balloon come down in flames. Very difficult to decide who has control of the air."

In an obituary announcement dated October 28, 1918, there was the shocking news to Bradenton readers that Lieutenant Fred D. Barker of that town had been killed by a shell explosion while working with other Red Cross volunteers to bury the dead at Saint Mihiel. Barker had given up a profitable law practice to volunteer his services on behalf of his country. He left behind a wife and three children, the eldest of whom was attending the naval academy at Annapolis. Barker's hometown journal, the *Manatee River Journal*, on November 28, 1918, published a letter to his sister, Mrs. Lovell Gates, dated September 18, 1918. In one of the more telling instances of the war, Barker related how he went to the front at the beginning of the "big drive" and found the local headquarters

> *The next day, the big drive started, and I never heard such a racket. About 5:30 a.m., I took thermos bottles of coffee up to the headquarters, which is in a cave in the side of a bluff, about 20 above ground. I crawled up and found the colonel alone sitting at the telephone....He invited me to sit down, and when the colonel invites, one sits. At 6, he had a few minutes and said, "I'm a bit tired and lonely. Won't you eat breakfast with me."...(We had finished what I had brought). So, on the morning of the great American drive, I had breakfast with the Colonel, off a soap box. We sat on straw on the ground, and the ground shook so from the jar of the guns that the dishes would hardly stay on the box.*

Lieutenant Barker then noted his own progress, "So, I left, and all day was busy at the hospital, or feeding men who had become separated from their rations. I was the muddiest, dirtiest mess you ever saw that night, and again slept in the dugout. The next morning, we loaded the little truck with food and smokes and started up." As noted earlier, he was killed serving his fellow soldiers and men—this was his last letter.

The next target on the route up the valley of the Meuse took the men by the point known as Montfaucon, a rather high point that allowed the German artillery and machine gunners to control the passage. The land had been churned up by countless shells, mines and bombs during the French offensive of 1916. Clair Jones and Will Austin took part in the campaign, and their unit was one of those charged with repairing the roadway around the infamous Le Homme Mort (Dead Man's Hill). The mud and rain made thorough repair almost impossible, but American inventiveness found a practical solution: "We do this by gathering stones from shell holes, carrying them in sandbags on our backs and then dumping them in the road. This operation is kept up day and night, fair weather or foul."

Will Austin wrote, "Clair and I are living on two slices of bacon, two slices of bread and a part of a small can of meat. And we have to go three miles for a canteen of water to make our coffee." The traffic picture was made worse by the American army moving east and the exhausted French troops, whom the Americans were replacing, going west to Paris, complete with the local refugees. Dead horses stacked along the side of the road gave off a stench that was anything but pleasant, and the landscape was a living nightmare with shell holes, gaping holes from mine explosions and the ruins of many small villages and towns. The boys went over the top at 5:30 a.m. on September 26 and laid down the chicken wire mesh and took out yard on yard of barbed wire with the Bangalore torpedoes. As members of the engineers' pioneer group, they were the first over the top and were the most exposed to the dangers lurking ahead.

The air war over the lines was a thing of interest to both the ground troops, who often depended on the flyers to provide information and drop bombs on the enemy during the battle, and the flyers themselves. Although

Harry Land of Bradenton in the Ninety-Fourth Aero Squadron "Hat in the Ring" airplane. *Courtesy of the Manatee County Public Library.*

the flyers have been heavily romanticized by authors and filmmakers, the reality for people like Manatee's Harry Land was something quite different. Land wrote a number of letters to the *Manatee River Journal* covering many facets of his training in Texas and his shipment overseas. However, the letters covering his time in the air over France are valuable for their perceptions and observations.

> *Another thing is that this front is creeping forward over the most battle-scarred and shell-torn of the whole line (around Verdun during the Meuse-Argonne Offensive), which has not moved in over four years of hard fighting. It is one shell hole merging into the next so that a forced landing is almost sure to mean a smashed plane. Had to make several trips over to see what I describe, as on the first trip, you don't see much. We first came to the balloon line, then the artillery, which was flashing very regularly, and as we pass, can hear the crack very plainly through the noise of our motors, and the explosions give our planes a decided lurch as we fly through the barrage of our side, with shells coming back from the other side. We have a good chance of being hit by either side. We then come to the trenches, which look like a nightmare from above, crocked and zigzagged without regard to direction. Then comes the enemy artillery and balloon Line, which is the eyes of the artillery as well as observation planes. These are "strafed," which is a very dangerous outdoor sport and will be described Later.*
>
> *In the meantime, we get "Archied" by the Black Archie (Boche), and on our side, we see several more white puffs of our Archie, which warns us that the Boches are coming. The sky is full of planes, French, American, British and German, and from a short distance in the air, they all look very much the same, and when you get close enough to make out the cockades, it is time to begin shooting, so we really have to be able to recognize the plane by the silhouette, which is very hard to do. When you get back, the old hands will say, "Did you see those Boches?" And I have to admit I thought they were some of our own planes, if I saw them at all.*

Land's letters offer an insight into the importance of the flyers in the overall scheme of battle, driving out machine gunners, locating enemy artillery and knocking down the spotting balloons were very crucial parts of the battle that often did not get reported.

The final major push of the war before the armistice came in the Meuse-Argonne, a desecrated landscape between the Meuse River and the Argonne Forest. The area had seen battles and skirmishes since the beginning of the war in 1914. Things were so chopped up that the hills received numbers, not names, and the valleys were still reeking of gas and cordite. Into this morass went Austin and Jones with the Sixth Engineers. Austin's informative diary tells much of the story beginning on October 13, 1918.

> *Left camp at 7:30 p.m., all those physically fit (150 men went, we were 100 men short). Marched to a point on the road near Mantilly and stayed for the night in low bushes by the roadside. There was a shell hole beside our tent about 30 feet across and 15 to 18 feet deep. Clair and I did not dig in on account of the roots, so when big shells came over, we thought we were "for it."*

The following day, the duo stayed put but ventured into no man's land for about a mile to get the lay of the land. "Our first duty was to bury the German and American dead and make the place sanitary." By October 18, the men were being shelled on a regular basis, and the crew lost six horses with the rest injured in one instance. On the following day, they were informed that the unit would fight as infantry in support of the Seventh Infantry Division, which was assigned the task of taking Hill 297 and Hill 299 by assault. On October 20, the men went over the top after fixing their trusty bayonets.

Austin's diary continued with the story of the Sixth Engineers' part in the Meuse-Argonne offensive.

> *Facing our foxholes was a long hill or "hog's back" covered with a fringe of woods on the summit. When we reached this point, we were surprised by a "hell" of machine gun bullets, which caused us to seek cover. Our captain learned that the big barrage by the American artillery, which was to have cleared the way for the infantry, had fallen short and the infantry had been almost annihilated. So now it was "up to us." We went forward, driving the Germans out of the Bois de Pultiere. By making a dash across an open field, we next gained the edge of the Clair Chenes woods. This woods was bristling with machine guns, and we had a hot time. Clair and I wondered what made the bullets snap so—some sounded like the crack of a whip while other seemed to moan. We discovered to our discomfort that the bullets that snapped were passing a few inches from our faces, while those that passed at a distance of five yards or more made the moaning sound.*

Under the threat of being surrounded by more than three hundred Germans who were then approaching the woods, the captain received orders to withdraw the men from this position. Austin's diary continued:

> *We withdrew in good order and the Germans seeing our design, sent up a flare signaling for a barrage. The reply was immediate. The 77s and one pounders dropped thick around us. As we were about to make a bayonet charge to clear away the few gunners that were between us and the hill (298) a shell came in. It hit the ground about 30 feet to our right, and the concussion nearly knocked us all down. While we lay waiting for the gas to clear so we could go on, I turned to look at Clair (there was just one man between us). His face was blank. I saw a piece of shrapnel had struck him in the temple. It had apparently gone straight to his brain. I watched him die.*

Austin and his remaining colleagues charged the hill but found the Germans had abandoned it to the Americans. It took six more days of very tough fighting to take the two remaining hills, 297 and 299. After his return stateside, Will Austin made a trip to Anna Maria Island and presented his mother with his diary.

The Meuse-Argonne campaign was a very brutal affair. For the forty-seven days of fighting, the costs to the AEF was around 117,000 casualties, while they inflicted over 100,000 casualties on the enemy. This figure included 26,000 prisoners of war taken. Some of these men were taken by the unit that included Sergeant Alvin York. York's platoon leader at the beginning of the campaign was another native of Manatee County, Kirby Pelot Stewart. Stewart had risen to the rank of lieutenant by the time of the attack that took his life. While leading the charge up Hill 228, the young lieutenant was shot in the legs by a German machine gun. He did not give up and began crawling up the hill, waving his 45 when another shot to his head instantly killed him. York and others of the command mourned his death and the loss of his leadership. In a 1984 *Bradenton Herald* feature piece, reporter Jay Greene interviewed some of the few surviving doughboys living in Manatee County. Doughboy Stan Zimowski noted the almost universal feeling of those who experienced the front-line action: "You never could tell if you were going to get hit when you were in the midst of it. Shells were dropping all around, men were falling everywhere, crying out in pain. I only had one thought in mind: to reach my objective."

The war engendered many bad feelings concerning the Germans, and the propaganda used by the committee for public information, headed by George Creel, often intensified these feelings. But not all harbored ill-will toward the German enemy. After all, their men were just like Americans; they were fighting for their country with no real questions about why they were doing so. The front-line troops who were in the trenches the day the armistice was signed were just happy the war was over. Jay Greene's interviews with the surviving doughboys included a statement by A.C. Smith that pretty much summed up their feelings: "We were never mad at the Germans, just with the Kaiser. We had heard such awful stories....Within two minutes after the fighting stopped, we were trading souvenirs with the Germans. They were sick of war, too." Not everyone had cause to celebrate on this occasion. "While standing on Central Avenue yesterday morning, rejoicing with the city at the coming of peace, Mrs. G.N. Moody of Eleventh street and Baum Avenue in St. Petersburg was handed a telegram announcing the death of her son in France. He died of pneumonia. The news was a terrible shock to the mother and friends had to assist her home."

8

FLORIDA'S PUBLIC HEALTH CRISIS

The 1918 Influenza Pandemic

The arrival of the novel coronavirus and the disease COVID-19 in China in 2019 and the pandemic that followed in 2020 removed the need to remind the public of the nature of viruses, their potential for combining bits of DNA and RNA to infect and multiply. This can be seen as a replay of what happened to the world in 1918 and 1919 but without twenty-first-century scientific knowledge and instant communication. And yet, the same "cures" are being offered, including social distancing, closing public venues, facemasks and numerous hopeful, but as yet unsuccessful, solutions.

Prior to the 1918–19 pandemic, influenza was not a reportable disease. Only in 1918 did influenza become recognized as a clinical disease. What was identified as "influenza" in the early twentieth century was the bacterium usually called Pfeiffer's bacillus. With the origin of the new killer unidentified, the public speculated Germany's wartime "devilishness" had somehow introduced it as part of a sabotage campaign. On October 12, 1918, the *Tallahassee Daily Democrat* ran a headline "Suspicion More Devilishness" and speculated, "With the Spanish influenza doing its worst in shipyards and camps, there comes an official assertion that it is possible the rapidly spreading disease was turned loose on these shores by German agents." This was not as illogical as it seems because they were sabotaging industry, shipping and livestock in an attempt to slow down or halt American aid to the Allies.

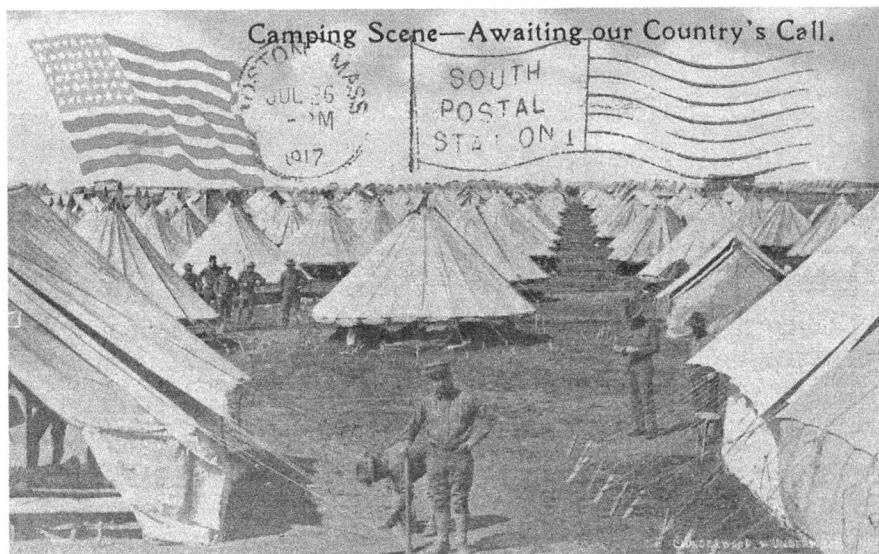

Camping scenes—awaiting our country's call. *Author's collection.*

What answers could be found to a limited degree awaited the invention of the electron microscope in 1933. Death records worldwide are generally estimated. The worldwide death toll was estimated to have reached 40 to 100 million, with the recorded U.S. death toll listed at around 675,000 by the end of 1919. Confusing the issue further was that many deaths caused by the lung damage from the 1918 influenza virus were actually attributed to subsequent infections and pneumonias.

When the United States entered World War I in 1917, Florida was a producer of citrus fruit, naval stores, cattle and winter vegetables. It had a long coastline with a good deal of shipping going into Tampa Bay as well as three U.S. naval bases at Pensacola on the Gulf of Mexico, Jacksonville on the Atlantic coast and Key West, the gateway to the Gulf and Caribbean. All were major ports of entry at the time.

While the "official" reports of influenza specify the years 1918 and 1919, it was certainly circulating earlier in the southern World War I wartime training camps. In Florida, there were 170 deaths attributed to influenza and pneumonia during 1917, with contagion probably entering the state at the wartime Jacksonville shipyards and the port. The disease reportedly killed at least 4,114 between September and December 1917 alone; this number was out of 13,155 persons recorded as having had "flu symptoms" for a recorded mortality rate of 31 percent.

Among the early 1917 deaths were Florida soldiers and family members. The *St. Petersburg Times* reported, "Eight More Die of Pneumonia Friday" at Camp Wheeler near Macon, Georgia, in a story dated November 30, 1917. The Florida boys were Houston Sanderlin of Lake City, Onley Roberts of Tulu and Silas Harrold of Wilburn, and they died along with four Georgia soldiers and one Alabama soldier, all stationed at Camp Wheeler. Thomas Drier of Jacksonville was reported to be a victim "of pneumonia" along with three Georgia boys at Camp Wheeler on December 4. Camp Wheeler was one of the major training bases for Florida troops headed to the war. In a related story from December 27, 1917, the *Manatee River Journal* reported that Mary L. Cram went to Camp Wheeler in Macon, Georgia, from Bradenton because her son Alanson was dangerously ill with pneumonia. She, too, was taken ill and died there on Christmas Day. Her son was carried to her bedside before she passed away.

In the Tampa Bay area, in Hillsborough County, including modern Pinellas, there were 518 deaths from influenza, or a combination of influenza and pneumonia, recorded. Manatee County, just south of Tampa Bay, still included modern Sarasota County and recorded 40 deaths. Inland, agricultural De Soto County, which then included Hardee County, reported a further 42 deaths. Florida was still a very rural state, and the area south of Tampa was hardly settled at all. South Florida was home to some of the

Our country is calling us. *Author's collection.*

Waldorf Astoria Hotel, the American Roentgen Society's goodbye dinner for physicians in uniform. *Author's collection.*

largest cattle ranches in the southern United States. Tampa, one of the more urban cities in Florida, had only just passed the 50,000 mark in population at the end of the war.

The problem of recording deaths was increased by the dearth of medical professionals, many of whom answered the nation's call when the U.S. Congress declared war. Doctors, nurses and any lady with Red Cross training were called on to serve in the army's woefully underprepared military training camps, aboard navy ships or in naval hospitals for service "over there" in France or Britain. Historian Carol Byerly has noted that nearly 30 percent of the physicians in America were in military service and that "there were sections of the country that were absolutely stripped of physicians." Additionally, "The exigencies of war also thwarted many of the efforts, such as crowd mitigation and quarantines to control the epidemic." Greatly reduced medical assistance, the war "exigencies" and general ignorance of the rural population all set the stage for a major disaster.

It may not have mattered very much if the doctors and nurses had all remained in Florida. No one knew about viruses. "Germ theory" had completely taken its place with wonderful results. Cholera, typhus, typhoid fever, dengue fever, yellow fever, whooping cough, mumps and more were known to be caused by germs. Your house would get the yellow Health Department quarantine notice nailed to your front door. The medieval idea of death from "miasmas" in the air had been discarded by the arrival of the microscope. American men who entered the woefully underprepared military training camps of World War I were

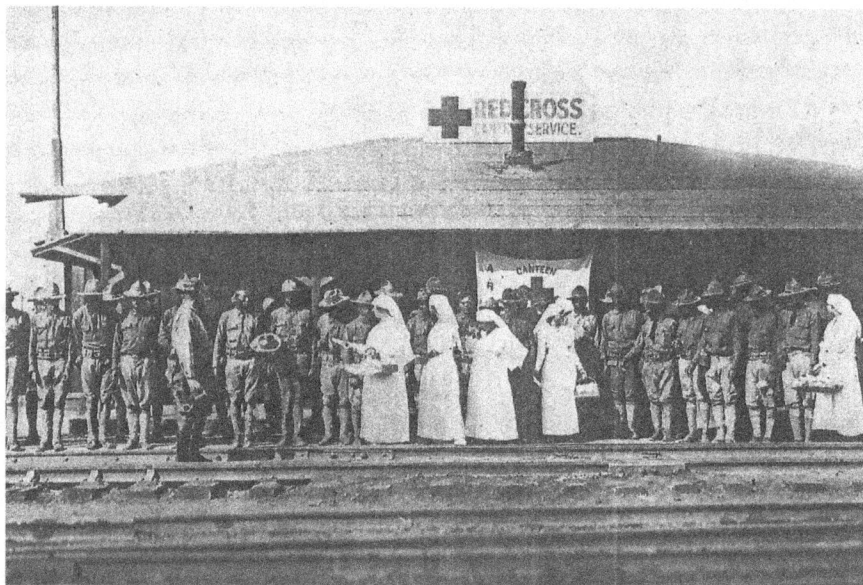

Red Cross nurses at a camp canteen near railroad tracks, circa 1917. *Author's collection.*

Nurses arriving in England on their way to France. *Author's collection.*

inoculated against everything except bullets, shrapnel, gas attacks and—oh, yes—syphilis. But influenza couldn't be found with a simple microscope and it acted as an airborne miasma.

Once the influenza damaged the victim's immune system, any other nearby germ was free to increase and multiply. Florida physicians encountered smallpox, typhoid fever, measles and diphtheria in the vicinity of rural Gadsden County alone. Three cases of scarlet fever were reported there as well. Gadsden was the center of shade tobacco production, which relied heavily on manual labor. Malaria was found in the Key West area, with one death, as well as nine cases of leprosy with one death. The navy encountered polio, tuberculosis, German measles and mumps. All of these diseases were thought to have been eliminated or greatly reduced by modern medicine.

The *St. Petersburg Times* reported an AP newswire story on July 30, 1918: "Would Prevent Influenza in All U.S. Shipyards. Health Authorities Act to Protect Men from Spanish Epidemic." Sanitation engineers were sent to all shipyards, which, in Florida, would include Jacksonville. Just three months later, on September 24, 1918, the *St. Petersburg Times* warned of "Spanish Influenza at 25 U.S. Army Camps." There were 20,000 total reported cases, with 2,225 new cases that day including Florida's Camp Joseph E. Johnston. Only two days later, on September 26, the *St. Petersburg Times* reported, "Rapid Spread of Spanish Flu Is Cause for Alarm." Only two days after the first report, 5,000 new cases had occurred in the twenty-five camps. By September 29, 6,824 new influenza cases had been reported.

Dr. William Warren, the state's district health officer for Key West and Monroe County, noted that the increased population of Key West by U.S. servicemen and the families of servicemen stationed there "required watchfulness on the part of the health authorities." The navy department's district sanitation officer for the Seventh Naval District, Dr. G.M. Guiteras, under the supervision of Admiral William B. Fletcher Sr., made a systematic inspection of the entire city to remove any source of "disease and nuisances." Yellow fever must have been the main fear, as they concentrated on screening all water containers and cesspools. The Spanish-American War experience was no doubt an undesirable memory. Nevertheless, influenza appeared among the navy personnel at both the training station and at the United States Marine Hospital. Dr. Warren reported that of the first twenty deaths from influenza in Monroe County, fourteen victims were servicemen and six were civilians.

American railroads and the government had learned from experiences in the Spanish-American War and the 1916 Mexican Border War and were better organized for dealing with World War I. They were actually working in defiance of the 1914–16 U.S.-declared status as a neutral power, and they planned how to prepare for men, building supplies, equipment, munitions and food, as well as how to deliver it effectively where it was needed. Led by competent railroad industrialists and government planners who could see clearly just how unprepared the United States was to fight a big war, they were ready to help America build its fighting force from the ground up and transport the men, equipment and food supplies to their debarkation points. Yet even with the expert planning and traffic controls, the sheer volume of traffic clogged the system near the port of New York, bringing delays and backups as bad as those in Tampa during the Spanish-American War. By early 1918, most of the problems had been worked out, including better coordination with the shipping firms and staggered debarkation times.

The only thing these planners didn't figure on was chicken pox, mumps, measles, diphtheria, pneumonia, strep and staph infections, Pfeiffer's influenza bacillus and an influenza virus, which would ride right along in those packed railroad cars with the soldiers and sailors. At recruiting centers and draft reporting centers, men who passed their physical exams were inoculated against most known communicable diseases—except viral infections. Today, with a flu shot, patients are told to go home, relax, drink

"Hello? Take my advice." *Author's collection.*

lots of fluids and keep moving so the vaccine can circulate throughout the body. In 1917 and 1918, soldiers were simply told to tote their packs, stand in line and get disinfected for lice to prevent typhus and get dressed. They were crammed into train cars and shipped to a camp. They had no way to relax, food and drink were likely to come at odd times—probably late—and sleep was for peacetime. Could this have overtaxed the young men's natural germ fighting abilities? New recruits and draftees came to the camps with lowered immune systems from fighting off the germs introduced by the vaccinations, and they were picking up every cold and virus that could be spread around the trains.

In World War I, the U.S. military lost roughly 53,500 men in combat-related deaths. While the pandemic was at its peak, the enormous numbers of victims affected made a scientific study of the character of the disease and any development of new approaches to prevention and treatment impossible. Influenza was described as explosive, with death sometimes occurring within two days of the onset of symptoms. From September 1 to October 31, 1918, the army medical department reported, "One out of every five soldiers stationed in the United States contracted the disease." Up to 40 percent of each mobilization and training camp was affected by influenza. Mild cases may have been misdiagnosed. Military medical personnel, exhausted, also fell victim to the flu. Of the approximately 621,000 soldiers and sailors who caught the flu, 43,000 died in 1918, a number equaling 80 percent of those 53,500 total combat deaths in the World War. By the end of the epidemic in 1919, a total of 57,000 had died of influenza and accompanying complications of pneumonia—more than the U.S. forces' total combat deaths.

Let the numbers tell the story. On November 1, 1918, the *Florida Times Union* ran a comparison of deaths reported to the City of Jacksonville's health department in 1917 and 1918. While the birth rate remained stable, influenza was listed as the main cause of death in October 1918. For white males, 170 died in 1918, as compared to only 39 the year before. White female deaths were up to 126 from 1917's 20. African American male deaths for 1918 were up to 122 from 53 in 1917. African American female deaths were up to 143 from only 20 in 1917. The deaths occurring at nearby Camp Joseph E. Johnston added an additional 155 deaths.

In 1918, at the University of Florida's crowded campus, the flu spread rapidly. President Murphree and hundreds of students fell ill. Math department head Professor H.G. Keppel passed away from the disease. The university's vice-president James Marion Farr directed the influenza campaign, with women from the Gainesville Red Cross and still-healthy students and faculty members helping. Beds had to be hauled from dormitories and over to a temporary hospital in the Floyd Griffin Agricultural Building. That crisis ended in a few weeks, but small outbreaks returned in 1919. The *St. Petersburg Times* was still following the story on October 1, when it reported that L.D. Childs sent an offer to nurse the stricken college men at the state university on learning there were eighty-five cases of influenza at the school. In the end, nearly 30 percent of the student body was affected by the influenza, and a number died. With the assistance and aid of the women of Gainesville, who washed clothing and sheets and provided healthy meals, the university pulled through. Many in the area, however, blamed the transfer of four hundred men to the campus for training for the outbreak of influenza. No one really questioned the need for the training in the national emergency.

At Tallahassee's Florida State College for Women, the *Tallahassee Daily Democrat* reported on October 12, 1918, "Flu at College Admirably Managed" and said, "As soon as the slightest symptoms develop, the patient is rushed in the infirmary and there given the best attention possible. In fact, the girls are far better treated than they would be in their homes." It is one of the only reports about the college to appear in the newspapers, and none of the histories of the school even mention the influenza outbreak in the state's capitol. The same can be said for the "colored" college, today's Florida Agricultural and Mechanical University.

Across the Atlantic, America's "big push" in the First World War came with the Meuse-Argonne offensive between September and November 1918. It was a brutal affair with huge casualties, more than any battle since the Civil War. Its total numbers were staggering for Americans: 17,647 killed, 69,833 wounded by gunfire or artillery shelling, 18,864 gassed, over 2,000 shell shocked and 68,760 hospitalized with medical problems, mostly influenza. Ten percent of the entire force were noted as "stragglers," and many of them were suffering from the effects of the influenza and were not reported. The influenza almost caused the entire offensive to collapse, bogging down troop movements, consuming medical and transportation resources and weakening the forces available to General Pershing, who may have suffered from the influenza himself; it also put a strain on all other resources. The impact on morale, although unmeasurable, was thought to have been significant. Men who were ready to go over the top looked behind to find men collapsing in the trenches from influenza, not enemy action. Pershing, with new troops headed for the front lines—many

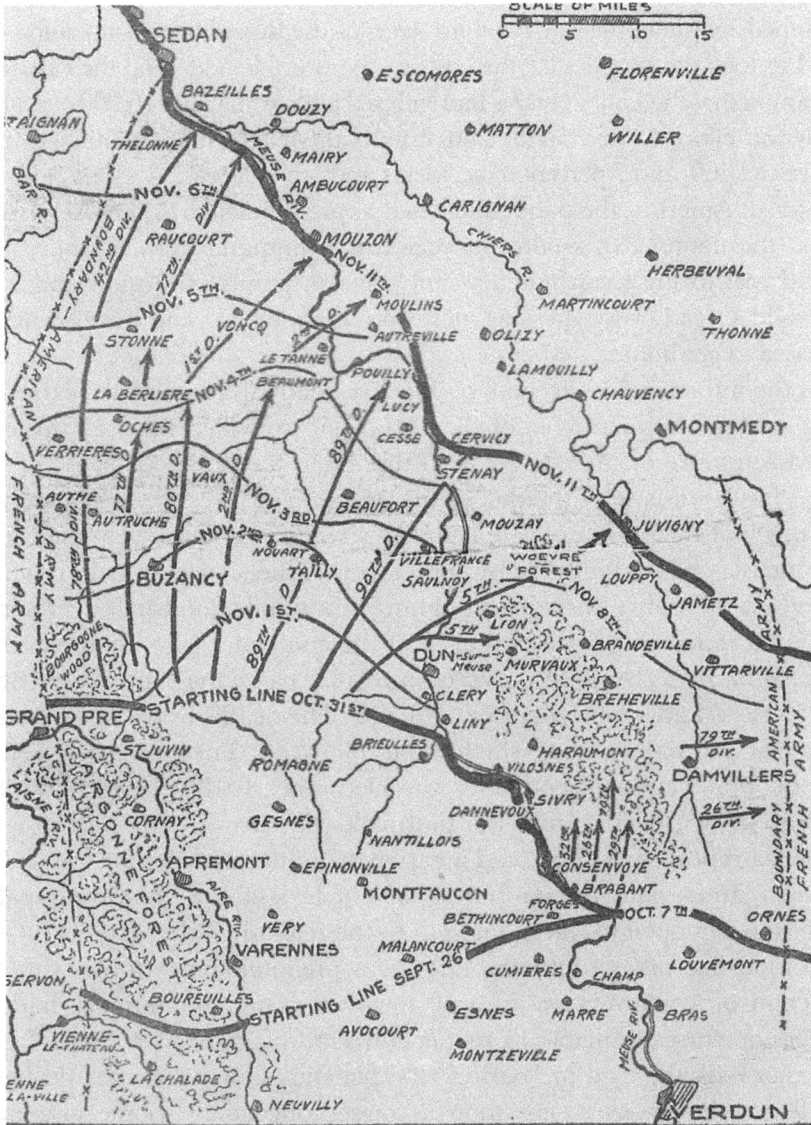

The Meuse-Argonne advance routes. *Author's collection.*

already infected by the virus—could not rely on the forces at hand or the replacements he desired. The Meuse-Argonne could have been a disaster of greater proportions, but luckily, the numbers available continued to grow despite the disease, and the American Expeditionary Force won its most important battle and helped end the war.

Immediately after the war, Leonard Ayers of the Russell Sage Foundation was asked to total the statistics for the costs of the war. He added up the casualties and found that the United States had suffered approximately 116,000 casualties in the war effort, 43 percent (50,280) from battle-related injuries, 50 percent to disease (57,460) and 7 percent to accidents and other causes.

Back in America, the pandemic killed approximately 675,000 Americans across the nation. No section or region was immune from the horror. It spread east to the main military embarkation points of Boston and New York and spread everywhere as men were demobilized and traveled across America to get home.

As the influenza hit the state of Florida, many were quick to blame the troop movements in and out of the port of Jacksonville. Although this may have been more of an exaggeration than fact, the port took some of the blame for the disease's spread. The transmission of the virus was unknown, and much of the press and people on the street simply guessed at the cause. Like measles, which hit the army and Florida earlier, it was an airborn virus, spread via breathing, sneezing, coughing or a simple handshake. Influenza was not a reportable disease until it hit the epidemic stage. By the end of 1918, after it was being reported on a regular basis, the state experienced 13,155 cases and a mortality rate of 4,114. The deaths were "attributed to influenza and pneumonia, which often followed." These numbers reflect only the time between September and December 1918. These are not the total of known deaths from the outbreak. There were 981 deaths from influenza reported in 1917, and a gap exists in the statistics for the period between January and September 1918. The lack of early reporting makes these statistics open to questioning as to the real toll in the state.

Florida, like other southern states, was predominantly rural. With the depletion of caregivers because of the war, many communities had no doctors or nurses available to render any kind of care. As a result, home remedies took the lead in "curing" the patients. Onions, garlic and herbs of all descriptions were common in these concoctions. Some employed incantations like, "Sour, sour vinegar v: keep the sickness off'n me," or other doggerel verse to fight the bug. In a day when families still buried their kinfolk in cemeteries on their own property, reporting deaths was not a priority. When Florida was finally accepted into the registration area for deaths and the records of the bureau of vital statistics near the end of 1918, the reliability of statistics improved dramatically. Any figures given prior to January 1, 1919, when the actual reporting began, would have to be speculative only and unreliable.

Getting physicians to the scene was problematic at best. Throughout the nation, the total number of registered physicians was listed at 140,000, and over 40,000 of them were enlisted in the nation's armed services at the beginning of the war. The constant calling for more trained doctors by the military put a strain on recruiting for areas such as Florida, where most of the physicians were clustered near the more urban areas. There were very few doctors in the rural areas, and many of them refused to treat African Americans, who relied on local sources and midwives for medical assistance. Nurses, too, were in short supply, and the Jacksonville district health officer, Dr. John Keely, noted this in his report, "I would like to emphasize the imperative need of nurses and assistants if this work [fighting influenza] is to be carried out properly." At the time, public health nurses were struggling to get professional recognition and adequate funding for their work. Getting nurses to the patients in rural areas was a real struggle, and automobiles were difficult for nurses to purchase. The state did have an allowance for such transportation; however, with the election of Sidney J. Catts as governor, that option was eliminated, something state health officer Dr. Joseph Y. Porter feared. The Red Cross, which selected the nurses for the army and navy, put advertisements and stories in the local press asking for nursing volunteers. In the *St. Petersburg Times* on October 5, 1918, the headline read, "Red Cross Seeking Nurses to Battle the Flu Epidemic." So desperate was this valuable organization that they would welcome women with any kind of training or experience in providing healthcare. It was dangerous work.

Doctors, too, were not immune to the disease—especially this strain of influenza. As Dr. Keely reported to Jacksonville, he had to take care of five of his colleagues. His counterpart in Tallahassee, Dr. L.T. Gilpin, reported, "On my arrival in Quincy, I found four of the five local physicians confined to bed with the flu, and the remaining one almost exhausted and with 1,200 cases of flue in town and the immediate vicinity." Civilian doctors recruited into the nation's service were from a variety of backgrounds, and many were from rural states like Florida. When the United States entered the war, it had approximately 26,000 doctors in its "medical reserve." Many of these doctors were either from rural areas with limited exposure to more modern medical methods or had a significant distrust of "laboratory scientists" who pushed the new medicine. Hence a number of these doctors were actually opposed to the medical practice of their more enlightened and experienced colleagues. Many of these gentlemen, it should be remembered, had graduated or entered practice in the 1880s or early 1890s and were often in remote locations, away from the new "real world" of modern medicine

Cora Davis and nurses at Gordon Keller Hospital in Tampa, Florida. *Courtesy of the Manatee County Public Library.*

in which germ theory was a given. Influenza challenged these men as no other disease could have, and some of them found the lessons costly—if not fatal. Historian George Culver used statistics from the American Medical Association and found that the influenza killed 428 physicians in 1918 and 313 in 1919. Simply put, no one was safe from influenza.

Florida was not alone in facing the epidemic and the extremely rapid spread of the disease. It surprised nearly everyone, including the Public Health Service (PHS), which had never seen anything this dangerous in its history. The PHS noted in its weekly report that Key West had reported a number of influenza cases among the military personnel stationed on the island on September 28, and by October 18, it noted the startling fact that in the space of eleven days (September 5 to September 15) 158 deaths had occurred and over 800 cases were reported among the civilian population of the island. In its October 25 report, the PHS noted 371 deaths, 234 of them in Jacksonville and 10 in Gainesville. Ironically, the thirteenth-annual report of the state board of health proudly noted that number of death certificates was greater for 1918 than 1917, but most of that was caused by the better registration, "as the so-called influenza is responsible for a large part of the difference."

Any travel, unless it was absolutely necessary, became very restricted and not just because of rationing. Some cities, like Jacksonville, attempted to quarantine, but that effort often failed. In the case of Jacksonville, a certain denizen of Ocala, known only as "Mr. Olsen," got by the quarantine not once but twice to do some carpentry work. On the second occasion, he returned to Ocala and spread the disease to his family and probably others. Luckily, none of his immediate family members died. The increase in ease of travel via trains and automobiles may have been a factor in spreading the disease. Public places such as movie theaters and dance halls were beginning to close their doors because customers feared infection. As the disease spread, cities and counties passed temporary ordinances closing these types of establishments and even went so far as to close schools and churches for the duration of the infection. According to research reported by Joann Schulte, all Florida schools were closed for three to four weeks to curb the spread of the disease. Manatee County closed its schools in early October, and the school board met in a special session to pass a resolution paying the county's schoolteachers for the two weeks lost in obedience to the order of the county health officer. Churches also closed during this time, and Judge O.K. Reaves had to shut down the circuit court because, of the eighteen people called to serve as jurors, ten were on military duty or other public cause, four had the influenza and only four remained to sit as a jury. The judge had little choice but to suspend court until "conditions become normal." Even Bradenton's *Manatee River Journal* nearly had to shut down in mid-October when the linotype operator came down with influenza. Luckily, the *Sarasota Times* came to the rescue, and the paper continued to provide the news.

The news the paper carried was not bright and cheery. As the war dragged on, casualties took the lives of some prominent men in the community. Lieutenant Fred D. Barker lost his life serving in the Red Cross while assisting in the burial of American soldiers. Lieutenant Kirby Pelot Stewart died while commanding troops during the Meuse-Argonne offensive. His unit suffered many deaths and casualties during the assault, including most of his sergeants, leaving command to other noncommissioned officers, including one Sergeant Alvin York of Stewart's platoon.

These stories added to the sadness of the community but were to be expected given the nature of the war. What was not expected was the large number of deaths from influenza. Lieutenant Wallace Lyverse was reported as seriously ill in Newport News, Virginia. His mother went to see him, and he died of pneumonia shortly after her arrival. Wannie Finch left Myacca

Brothers John and Lieutenant Kirby Pelot Stewart. *Courtesy of the Manatee County Public Library.*

for his military duties at Southern College but died before his first full week was completed. Major Edgar M. Graham of the quartermaster's corps died in France from pneumonia following a short bout with the influenza. His wife and children had just moved to Kentucky to be with family while the major was on active duty. Another victim was Frederick at Hampton Roads. According to the account of his death, he succumbed to pneumonia after a

Nellie Abbe (Mrs. F.C.) Whitaker, a Sarasota pioneer. *Courtesy of the Manatee County Public Library.*

short bout with influenza. His mother made it to his bedside in time to offer some last-minute comfort.

The news reported on the home front was often not better. Palmetto lost one of its leading lights, Professor C.T. Dickie, a member of the school board and long-time associate with the Palmetto Drug Company who died of influenza in late October. Laura Bessie Calhoun, a schoolteacher at Roser School in St. Petersburg, also succumbed in early December. She was twenty-one years of age. Mrs. F.C. Whitaker died in Cleveland, Ohio, in mid-November after leaving Bradenton with her husband, Dr. F.C. Whitaker, for a trip to Massachusetts, where his son, who was also a doctor, had left his practice to join the medical corps. Within a week of reaching Massachusetts, Mrs. Whitaker was called to Cleveland to care for her daughter's family, who had taken ill with the flu. She, herself, was quickly stricken and died in her daughter's home. Stories like these filled the newspapers of the day and cast a pall over the land. No one, it appeared, was immune.

In John Berry's excellent account *The Great Influenza: The Story of the Deadliest Pandemic in History*, he correctly noted, "In every war in American history so far, disease has killed more soldiers than combat. In many wars, throughout history, war had spread disease." American medical leaders had anticipated that a major epidemic could arise from the war and prepared as well as they could for such an event. All they could do was wait for it to strike. A classic example of the thing they feared came with the Eighty-Eighth Division, which went to France in September 1918, poorly trained and devoid of complete medical staff. They were immediately sent to the front and suffered horribly, with 90 men killed, wounded or captured. They lost 444 to influenza.

Despite the epidemic that so weakened the American army, the enemy was also struck by influenza, and General Erich von Ludendorff noted after the war, "Our army suffered. Influenza was rampant....It was a grievous business having to listen every morning to the chiefs of staff's recital of the number of influenza cases and their complaints about the weakness of the troops if the English attacked again." This weakness feared by the German commanders and the large number of American soldiers who could be thrown against them in growing numbers with each passing month was a decisive factor in Germany agreeing to an armistice. If Ludendorff had known that chief of staff Payton March had reported to Pershing a 20 percent illness rate among the troops getting ready to embark for France and the fact that the draft had been stopped by the influenza, he might have reconsidered, but that is doubtful given the spread of the disease among the German army and the starvation rates at home due to the British blockade. Since all sides were suffering from the pandemic and Germany was starving and on the edge of revolution, the armistice was the only practical move to be made. Historian Richard Collier best described the irony of the event when he noted that the war had ended but had "ushered in the greatest medical holocaust in history."

General Payton March, the U.S. chief of staff. *Author's collection.*

It also ushered in the 1920s, the "Lost Generation" and a lack of writing that noted the passing of this greatest of all pandemics. It was if the country wanted to ignore the consequences of this dreaded disease and what it had done to over 675,000 fellow Americans. Among the number who died from the consequences of the disease, according to John Berry's study, was the president of the United States, Woodrow Wilson. Berry makes a very strong case that he did not suffer a stroke but was the victim of influenza. The pandemic was still active in Paris when he was there negotiating the Treaty of Versailles; almost his entire team, including daughter Margaret and wife, Edith, contracted it, as did chief White House usher, Irwin Hoover, and his personal physician, Dr. Gary Grayson. Given the highly contagious nature of the disease, there can be little doubt he contracted it. Grayson dutifully recorded his confinement to bed for over five days and his high fevers that reached 103 degrees Fahrenheit. His debilitated body simply could not stand up to the rigors of the negotiations, which were intense and acrimonious. In the end, he gave in to most of the demands of the French leader, George Clémenceau, including a demilitarized Rhineland, returning Alsace and Lorraine to France and paying of the crippling war reparations. There is little wonder that British economist John Maynard Keynes called him "the greatest fraud on earth." Most of the grand designs he had skillfully drafted in the famous "Fourteen Points" went out the window along with "the little bird whose name was Enza." Berry makes it clear, in his mind, that Wilson had influenza and only that. Weakened by the disabling effects of the disease, he could not stand up to the campaign to push for the treaty or the United States' entry into the League of Nations. America may have forgotten the Pandemic of 1918 in its history books, but the impact is written on almost every page after that date.

SUGGESTED READINGS

Ardalan, Christine. *The Public Health Nurses of Jim Crow Florida.* Gainesville: University Press of Florida, 2019.

Barry, John M. *The Great Influenza: The Story of the Deadliest Pandemic in History.* New York: Penguin Books, 2005.

Blum, Howard. *Dark Invasion, 1915: Germany's Secret War and the Hunt for the First Terrorist Cell in America.* New York: HarperCollins, 2014.

Breemer, Jan S. *Defeating the U-Boat: Inventing Antisubmarine Warfare.* Annapolis, MD: Naval Institute Press, 2010.

Brown, Warren. *Florida's Aviation History: The First Hundred Years.* Largo, FL: Areo-Medical Consultants Inc., 1994.

Byerly, Carol R. *Fever of War: The Influenza Epidemic in the U.S. Army during World War I.* New York: New York University Press, 2005.

Campell, James B. "Origins of Aerial Photographic Interpretation, U.S. Army, 1916–1918." *Photogrammetric Engineering & Remote Sensing* 74, 43 (January 2008): 77–93.

Child, Clifton J. "German-American Attempts to Prevent the Exportation of Munitions of War, 1914–1915." *Mississippi Valley Historical Review* 25, (December 1938): 351–68.

Collier, Richard. *The Plague of the Spanish Lady: The Influenza Pandemic of 1918–1919.* New York: Atheneum Books, 1974.

Cox, Francis. "The First World War: Disease, the Only Victor." Transcript, London: Museum of London, March 10, 2014.

Crosby, Alfred. *America's Forgotten Pandemic: The Influenza of 1918.* New York: Cambridge University Press, 1989.

Esterquist, Ralph T. "War Attitudes and Activities of American Libraries, 1914–1918." *Wilson Library Bulletin* 15 (April 1941): 623–36.

Foulois, Benjamin D. *From the Wright Brothers to the Astronauts: The Memoirs of Major General Benjamin D. Foulois.* New York: McGraw-Hill Book Company, 1960.

Greeley, William B., and George T. Morgan Jr., ed. "A Forester at War: Excerpts from the Diaries of Colonel William B. Greeley." *Forest History* (Winter 1961).

Gutherie, John D., et al. "The Carpathians." Tenth Engineers (Forestry) AEF, 1917–1919. Roster and historical sketch. Washington, D.C. May 1940.

Halpern, Paul G. *A Naval History of World War I.* Annapolis, MD: Naval Institute Press, 1994.

Jones, Jerry W. "U.S. Battleship Operations in World War I, 1917–1918." Doctoral dissertation, University of North Texas, October 1995.

Kalata, Gina. *The Story of the Great Influenza Pandemic of 1918 and the Search for the Virus That Caused It.* New York: Farrar, Straus and Giroux, 1999.

Koenig, Robert. *The Fourth Horseman: One Man's Mission to Wage the Great War in America.* New York: Public Affairs and Perseus Group, 2006.

Kosta, Del. "Air Reconnaissance in World War One." Military History Online. www.militaryhistoryonline.com.

Miller, Gordon K. *A Biographical Sketch of Major Edward E. Hartwick.* Detroit, MI: N.p., 1921.

Morison, Elting. *Admiral Sims and the Modern American Navy.* Boston: Houghton Mifflin Company, 1942.

Ridsdale, Percival. "How the American Army Got Its Wood." *American Forestry* 25, no. 2 (June 1929): 1,137–54.

Ripley, Peter C. "Intervention and Reaction: Florida Newspapers and the United States Entry in World War I." *Florida Historical Quarterly* 49, no. 3 (1971).

Schulte, Joann. "The 1918 Influenza Epidemic in Florida: An Historical Perspective." Florida Department of Health. www.doh.state.fl.us.

Simpson, Michael. "Admiral William S. Sims, U.S. Navy and Admiral Sir Lewis Bayly, Royal Navy: An Unlikely Friendship and Anglo-American Cooperation, 1917–1919." *Naval War College Review* 41, no. 3 (Spring 1988): 1–15.

Urlich, Carol. *The Role of the Library in Public Opinion Formation during World War I.* Minneapolis: University of Minnesota Press, 1971.

Warner, Michael. "The Kaiser Sows Destruction: Protecting the Homeland the First Time Around." Central Intelligence Agency. www.cia.gov.

Weigand, Wayne A. *An Active Instrument for Propaganda: The American Public Library during World War I.* Greenwood, NY: Greenwood Press, 1959.

Witcover, Jules. *Sabotage at Black Tom: Imperial Germany's Secret War in America, 1914–1917.* Chapel Hill, NC: Algonquin Books of Chapel Hill, 1989.

ABOUT THE AUTHORS

Dr. Joe Knetsch is the author of over two hundred articles and twelve books concerning Florida history. This is his sixth book for Arcadia Publishing and The History Press, and it covers an area he in which he has had a strong interest. He has been a constant reviewer of military history books for the *Journal of America's Military Past* and other professional journals. He holds a doctorate from Florida State University and was, for twenty-eight years, the historian for the Division of State Lands in the Florida Department of Environmental Protection. Since his retirement, he has continued to research and publish history pieces. He currently lives in Tallahassee with his wife, Linda, and their five cats.

Pamela N. Gibson is a Florida and local history specialist, recently retired from the Manatee County Public Library System after over forty-three years of service. There, she was in charge of the Eaton Florida History Collection. She has her master's degree in history from the University of South Florida.

She has published in *Sunland Tribune*, *Tampa Bay History* and *Professional Surveyor*, usually as coauthor with Dr. Joe Knetsch. Her research aid has been noted in the acknowledgements of a number of Florida history publications. She currently lives in Bradenton.